ROUTLEDGE LIBRARY EDITIONS:
. ENVIRONMENTAL AND NATURAL
RESOURCE ECONOMICS

Volume 6

OPTIMAL ECONOMIC GROWTH WITH EXHAUSTIBLE RESOURCES

OPTIMAL ECONOMIC GROWTH WITH EXHAUSTIBLE RESOURCES

PREM C. GARG

Routledge
Taylor & Francis Group

LONDON AND NEW YORK

First published in 1979 by Garland Publishing, Inc.

This edition first published in 2018
by Routledge
2 Park Square, Milton Park, Abingdon, Oxon OX14 4RN

and by Routledge
711 Third Avenue, New York, NY 10017

Routledge is an imprint of the Taylor & Francis Group, an informa business

British Library Cataloguing in Publication Data
A catalogue record for this book is available from the British Library

ISBN: 978-1-138-08283-0 (Set)
ISBN: 978-1-315-14775-8 (Set) (ebk)
ISBN: 978-1-138-10315-3 (Volume 6) (hbk)
ISBN: 978-1-315-10295-5 (Volume 6) (ebk)

Optimal Economic Growth with Exhaustible Resources

Prem C. Garg

Garland Publishing, Inc.
New York & London, 1979

Library of Congress Cataloging in Publication Data

Garg, Prem C   1946–
  Optimal economic growth with exhaustible resources.

  (Outstanding dissertations in economics) (Outstanding
dissertations on energy)
  Originally presented as the author's thesis, Stanford
University, 1974.
  Bibliography: p.
  1. Economic development—Mathematical models.
I. Title.   II. Series.   III. Series: Outstanding dissertations
on energy.
HD82.G27 1979   338.9'001'5   78-75019
ISBN 0-8240-4054-6

All volumes in this series are printed on acid-free,
250-year-life paper.
Printed in the United States of America

Acknowledgements

I am deeply in debt to Professor James L. Sweeney for his valuable guidance and encouragement during the course of this dissertation. I have also benefited from the comments and suggestions made by Professors Dimitri Bertsekas, Karl Shell and Edward Sondik. Messers Carson Agnew, Richard Gilbert and Robert Marks were also generous with their comments on the preliminary draft of this dissertation.

I am also thankful to Mr. A. Golan of the World Bank who kindly permitted me to take time off from my job for preparing this manuscript.

Finally, I am specially thankful to my friend, Christine, who showed an interest in this study which almost equalled mine.

Typing for this manuscript was done by Mrs. Dorothy Gundy. The research for this study was partially supported by The National Science Foundation through Grant GK 29237.

TABLE OF CONTENTS

LIST OF TABLES

LIST OF FIGURES

CHAPTER I

INTRODUCTION AND OVERVIEW

1.1 Introduction and Scope of the Study

In a controversial book, first published in 1798, Thomas Malthus postulated the prospects of a geometrically increasing population outstripping the limited natural resources of the earth. The subsequent turn of events in the wake of the industrial revolution, proved his analysis to be overly pessimistic. Nevertheless, the Malthusian spectre, in one form or another, has continued to be a source of concern and disagreement since then.[1] Over time Malthus' original emphasis on the availability of agricultural land has been expanded to include, among other things, the availability of exhaustible resources such as fossil fuels and mineral deposits. The latter issue has been a subject of vigorous debate between the economists and the conservationists for the past few years.

The conservationists have contended that the continuation of the current usage trends in exhaustible resources will lead to a catastrophic shortage in the near future.[2] The economists have scoffed at

---

[1] Vast amount of literature exists, much of it by non-economists, which either expands on Malthus' thesis or questions its validity. Barnett and Morse [5] provide a comprehensive review of the writing in this area.

[2] Most vocal expression of this concern, in recent days, are the two well-publicized studies: The Limits of Growth [20] and A Blueprint for Survival [1]. A Blueprint for Survival, for instance, is prefaced with the belief that "... if current trends are allowed to persist, the breakdown of society and the irreversible disruption of the life-support systems on this planet, possible by the end of this century, certainly within the lifetime of our children, are inevitable". The response to these two studies has been rather mixed. The Limits to Growth, for example, has been variously reviewed as "one of the most important documents of our age" [18] and as "an empty and misleading work" [24]. For

such suggestions arguing that any resource scarcity will be forestalled
by changes in tastes and technology, induced by the appropriate price
signals.[3]

Largely overlooked but central to the controversy is the issue
of inter-generational equity. Implicit in the conservationist concern
about the future availiability of exhaustible resources is the belief in
their inter-temporal misallocation, and particularly the belief that the
current usage trends 'unfairly' favor the present generation at the cost
of the future generations. Thus, at the heart of the controversy are the
questions such as: How should a society use its exhaustible resources
over time? What factors influence the usage pattern? Under what conditions is it optimal to exhaust the resources in a finite time? And
what role do these resources play in the overall growth of an economy?

This study is an attempt to develop a theoretical framework
for analyzing some of these issues. We explicitly introduce a homogenous
exhaustible resource in the aggregative production function of the society
and then, using the optimal growth theory framework, we analyze the

---

more substantive critiques of such studies see Cole [9] and Nordhaus [21].

[3]For instance, Barnett and Morse [5] after analyzing the resource
availability in the United States over the period 1870-1957 conclude that
"...the increasing scarcity of particular resources fosters discovery or
development of alternative resources, not only equal in economic quality
but often superior to those replaced."
See also Nordhaus and Tobin [23] who on the basis of falling share
of natural resource owners in national income, and some simulation exer-
cises conclude that either the elasticity of substitution between natural
resources and other factors of productions is high or technical change
is relatively resource-augmenting or both.
For a case study of the adaptive mechanism in handling a resource
scarcity see Rosenberg [30] who traces the historical trends in prices
of timber resources and the responses which they drew.

problem of optimally allocating a finite stock of the resource over time. In the process we point out the crucial parameters and value judgments relevant to the various issues. To underline the role played by exhaustible resource, the optimal behavior of the economy in our formulation is compared with that in the traditional formulation of the optimal growth problem.[4]

In a departure from most of the existing optimal growth theory literature, we analyse the problem for both the utilitarian and the max-min type criteria functional. The results for the two criteria are compared to evaluate their suitability for use in optimal growth models.

At places using some plausible values for the various parameters we speculate about the relevance of some of our results to the real world. The reader is cautioned, however, to treat the numerical examples as illustrations rather than as assertions.

1.2 A Survey of the Existing Literature

Considering the long standing nature of the controversy and considering the importance attached to the issue by the public in general, the available economic literature addressed to the problems of optimal inter-temporal usage of exhaustible resources is surprisingly small.

Of the limited literature which does exist, a large part is an outgrowth of a pioneering contribution by Hotelling [12]. Assuming an exogenously specified demand function, Hotelling analyses the problem of allocating over time a given stock of an exhaustible resource. He shows

---

[4]See for example Cass [7], Arrow and Kurz [4], Shell [34] or Intriligator [13].

3

that the profit maximizing owners of an exhaustible resource, facing a competitive situation will adjust the usage rate r(t) such that the resource price p(t) satisfies

$$p(t) = p(0) \cdot e^{\delta t}$$

where δ is the interest rate and p(0) is the initial price chosen so as to synchronize the exhaustion of the resource with the attainment of a price at which there is no demand.[5]

His results have been extended by a number of other researchers, to take into account some of the characteristics peculiar to the production in the extractive resource industries.[6] All of them however, have retained Hotelling's assumption regarding exogenous specification of the demand function.

Hotelling's contribution and the contributions following him are undoubtedly important in understanding the behaviour of firms in mineral industries. At the macro level however, the assumption of exogenous demand specification completely side-steps the central issue.

The problem of finding the optimal resource usage pattern at the macro level is complicated by the fact that if exhaustible resources are important to the production capabilities of an economy then resource usage decisions are inter-dependent with capital investment decisions e.g., the current resource usage rate influences the current output as well as the marginal productivity of capital. That in turn, influences

---

[5]It should be noted that price p is net of any extraction costs; it represents the opportunity cost only.

[6]See for example Gordon [10], Herfindahl [11], Scott [31], Burt and Cummings [6] and Sweeney [39].

4

the level of investment in the economy. On the other hand the current

capital stock, a result of past investment decisions, influences the

marginal productivity of the resources and hence their usage rate. Thus,

the resource usage decisions cannot be analyzed in isolation from the

rest of the economy-- indicating a need for an optimal growth theory

framework.

Contrary to what one might expect the existing economic litera-

ture on optimal growth theory has almost completely ignored the role of

exhaustible resources in the production process. The Solow [35], Swan

[38] neo-classical production function central to many of the optimal

growth models, uses only two kinds of inputs: labor and capital-- the

first one reproduces itself and the second one can be augmented through

production. A few exceptions to this general trend are the recent contri-

butions by Vousden [41], Koopmans [17], Anderson [3] and Solow [37].[7]

In Vousden the only factors of production acknowledged explic-

itly are the exhaustible natural resources; through such an extreme view

his analysis misses the essential interaction between the investment

decisions and the resource usage decisions. To a smaller degree the same

criticism applies to Koopmans' work in which it is assumed, in effect,

that the production from the natural resources can not be invested and

must be used for consumption only. Despite the limitations of their

models some of their conclusions are quite interesting. For example, it

---

[7]It ought to be noted here that during the past few years this area
has attracted considerable attention from researchers all over the world.
It is possible that many more studies may already be underway.

easily follows from Vousden's results that if exhaustible resources are
essential to production and if the marginal utility of consumption goes
unbounded as consumption approaches zero,then the exploitation of the
resources should be spread over an infinite time. Similarly Koopmans
shows that over time the shadow price of the resource relative to that
of the consumption good grows approximately at an exponential rate. As
we shall see later on,both these results are particular cases of our more
general results.

Anderson's work is apparently the first attempt, in
optimal growth theory literature, to use exhaustible resources in con-
junction with the two traditional inputs of capital and labor. He assumes that capital and labor combine together, in the neo-classical
fashion, to produce an intermediate output. This output is then combined
with a depletable resource to give the final output. Assuming the usual
relationships among consumption, investment and output, he analyses the
problem of optimal growth in a finite horizon setting. He concludes that
when exhaustible resources are incorporated into an optimal growth model,
the result is a tendency to use capital less intensively (i.e., a lower
capital-labor ratio and a lower saving rate) than in a non-resource
constrained model. The major shortcomings of his formulation are the
following three assumptions in his model:

* He assumes a fixed proportion production function vis-a-vis the
  depletable input and accordingly, there are no substitution possibilities between the exhaustible resources on the one hand and
  capital and labor on the other.

* Because of the finite horizon used in his model it is necessary
  to impose an arbitrary terminal constraint on the stock of the
  exhaustible resources.

6

* By using a utility function linear in consumption he misses some
   of the interesting interaction between the egalitarian bias of
   the society and the optimal resource usage pattern.

Later on in this study we shall show that his conclusion about
reduction of capital intensity depends crucially on his assumptions and
is not valid in general.

Solow's formulation is perhaps the best so far. He uses a
Cobb-Douglas production function and an infinite time horizon thus,
avoiding two of the shortcomings of Anderson's model. However, his main
concern in that work is to evaluate the suitability of the max-min
criterion for use in optimal growth models. His interest in the problems
of optimal resource exhaustion is tangential.[8]

In summary, the existing literature on optimal inter-temporal
usage of exaustible resources is barely off the ground and considerable
effort would be required before we have an adequate understanding of the
problem.

1.3 An Overview of the Study

Chapter II of this study discusses the formulation of the problem in its general form. The production rate of the economy is assumed
to be function of three homogenous factors-- the capital stock, the labor
supply and the usage rate of an exhaustible resource. In the neo-classical fashion, the production function is assumed to be continous, twice
differentiable and strictly concave. To the usual relationships among
capital, consumption, investment and output we add the constraint of a

---

[8]We shall refer to Solow's work in more detail in Chapter IV where
we extend his analysis and examine some of his results.

finite resource stock. Given initial stocks of the capital and the
resource, the objective is to maximize a discounted flow of utilities
over time, by choosing feasible consumption and resource usage trajectories.
Optimality conditions are derived and anlayzed for their economic interpretation. Also analyzed are the conditions necessary to ensure that the
resource will be exhausted over an infinitely long time.

     In Chapter III we present a detailed analysis of the optimal
growth paths assuming a Cobb-Douglas production function and an iso-
elastic utility function. We show that a set of initial conditions exists
from which the optimal solution is of a particularly simple form-- along
such a solution, capital, consumption and output all change at the same
exponential rate; the savings rate remains constant and the resource usage
rate declines exponentially. We show further that the optimal solution
starting from any other initial condition eventually converges to this
simple solution. It is shown that this special set of initial conditions
provides a simple way to determine whether an economy is relatively better
endowed with capital or with exhaustible resources.

     The optimal trajectories corresponding to arbitrary initial
endowments are analyzed in detail. The important role played by some of
the model parameters is examined. To emphasize the role of exhaustible
resources, the results are compared with those corresponding to the traditional formulation of the optimal growth problem. Numerical examples are
presented to illustrate the main analytical results.

     The model is then extended to incorporate technical progress.
The results are compared with the static technology case to bring out the
crucial importance of technical progress. It is shown that there exists

a minimum critical rate of technical progress such that if the actual progress rate were to exceed that rate then the economy could sustain an ever improving standard of living, despite the limitations imposed by the finiteness of the resource stock.

In Chapter IV it is shown that the analysis of Chapter III can be easily extended to the case where the social criterion functional is of the max-min type. It is shown that the use of the max-min criterion in our formulation merely implies the use of some specific values for the social discount rate and the elasticity of marginal utility of consumption. The results are discussed to compare the relative merits of using the utilitarian of the max-min criterion in optimal growth models.

Lastly, Chapter V provides a summary and discussion of the main conclusions of the study. Also discussed are the directions for future research, empirical as well as theoretical, needed for further illumination of the issues related to the use of exhaustible resources.

CHAPTER II

MODEL DESCRIPTION AND OPTIMALITY CONDITIONS

2.1 Model Description

Let the total production rate of the economy at time t be described by a constant returns to scale production function

$$Y(t) = Y(K(t), L(t), R(t)) \qquad (2.1)$$

in which to the two traditional inputs capital K and labor L, we have added a third input, the usage rate of the exhaustible resource R .

The output Y can be either consumed or invested i.e.,

$$Y = C + I \qquad (2.2)$$

where C and I are the consumption and investment flows, respectively. Assuming μ to be the rate of exponential depreciation of capital, the rate of capital formation $\dot{K}$ is given by

$$\dot{K} = I - \mu K \qquad (2.3)$$

Additionally, we assume that at the start of the plan, the total stock of the exhaustible resource is known with certainty to be X_0, and this sets the upper limit on the total use of the resource over time,[1] i.e.,

$$\int_0^\infty R \, dt \le X_0 \qquad (2.4)$$

---

[1]For simplicity, we exclude the possibility of any recycling; this can, however, be easily introduced into the model.

Defining $X(t)$ to be the resource stock remaining unused at time t, we can express (2.4) as

$$\left. \begin{array}{c} \dot{X}(t) = - R(t) \quad \text{with} \quad X(0) = X_0 \\ \text{and} \quad X(\infty) \geq 0 \end{array} \right\} \qquad (2.5)$$

Assuming that the labor force grows at a constant proportional rate n, the labor supply at time t will be given by

$$L(t) = L_0 \cdot e^{nt} \qquad (2.6)$$

where L_0 represents the initial labor force.

The constant returns to scale assumption together with (2.6) allows us to express the previous relations as

$$\left. \begin{array}{ll} \dot{k} = y(k,r) - (\mu + n)k - c & \text{(a)} \\ \dot{x} = - (r + nx) & \text{(b)} \end{array} \right\} \qquad (2.7)$$

and

where $y, k, r, c,$ and x are respectively the per capita quantities, restricted to be non-negative.

In the neo-classical fashion we assume y to be a twice differentiable concave function with positive and diminishing marginal products for all positive factor input levels i.e., for $k > 0, r > 0$:

$$\left. \begin{array}{ll} \dfrac{\partial y}{\partial k} > 0 \;, & \dfrac{\partial y}{\partial r} > 0 \\[2mm] \dfrac{\partial^2 y}{\partial k^2} < 0 \;, & \dfrac{\partial^2 y}{\partial r^2} < 0 \end{array} \right\} \qquad (2.8)$$

and

Also we assume that for $r > 0$

11

$$\left.\begin{array}{ll} \lim_{k \to 0} y(k,r) = 0 \quad , & \lim_{k \to \infty} y(k,r) = \infty \\[2em] \lim_{k \to 0} \frac{\partial y(k,r)}{\partial k} = \infty \quad , & \lim_{k \to \infty} \frac{\partial y(k,r)}{\partial k} = 0 \end{array}\right\}$$

and $\qquad\qquad\qquad\qquad\qquad\qquad\qquad\qquad\qquad$ (2.9)

Specifying the behaviour of y for limiting values of r, particularly for $r \to 0$, is more problematic. Depending upon how important a role one assigns to the exhaustible resources, a variety of assumptions are possible. One may take the implicit neo-classical view that these resources are not essential to production so that when the usage rate approaches zero, the output approaches some positive limit. Alternatively, one can take the conservationist view that no production is possible without these resources so that in the limit, the output approaches zero. Similarly one may assume that their marginal product either approaches a finite limit or, as for capital, becomes unbounded as the usage rate goes to zero. Conceivably, one could assume any of the four combinations. For the time being, we shall leave this limiting behaviour undefined.

Given some initial value of per capita stock $k(0) = k_0$ and the exhaustible resource endowment $x(0) = x_0$, the planning problem in the above setting is to choose the consumtion trajectory $c(t)$ and the resource usage rate $r(t)$, such that some criteria functional of the consumption stream is maximized.

The choice of the criteria functional, to a certain extent, is arbitrary, and there exists considerable disagreement, in economic

12

literature on optimal growth theory, about the appropriate form.[2] For
the time being, in line with the utilitarian approach, we shall assume
the welfare functional to be

$$W = \int_0^\infty e^{-\delta t} L(t) u(c(t)) \, dt \qquad (2.10)$$

where $\delta > 0$ is the subjective rate of time preference for discounting
future utilities.[3]

The utility function $u(\cdot)$ is assumed to be time invariant
and twice differentiable. Furthermore, for all $c \geq 0$

$$u'(c) > 0 \quad \text{and} \quad u''(c) < 0 \qquad (2.11)$$

---

[2]The disagreement originates primarily from two sources: first at
what rate, if at all, should the future utilities be discounted? In the
past, a number of noted economists, among them Pigou [25] and Ramsey [27],
have questioned the ethics of discounting future utilities in inter-
temporal comparisons. They felt that this discriminated against the un-
born future generations and blamed it on the 'defective telescopic
faculty of the human mind'. Presently the predominant opinion is in
favor of using positive discount rates. In part, this is justified by
the desire to recognize the consumer sovereignty in inter-temporal decisions at par with that for the decisions in a static setting. Another
part of the justification, however, is just the fact that mathematical
tractibility often dictates the use of positive discount rates.
      The second area of disagreement relates to the shape of the
social utility curve, i.e., should the utility function be based upon
total consumption or per capita consumption. Should it have a saturation
point? How large should the elasticity of marginal utility of consumption
be? (As we shall see later on, the magnitude of this elasticity has
some rather interesting implications for the optimal behavior, in the
present framework.)   See Chakarvarty [8] for a comprehensive discussion
of these points, and Arrow and Kurz [4] for a tentative justification
of the welfare functional in (2.10). For a contrary view, see Rawls
[28].

[3]Later on we shall see that δ would have to be constrained even
further.

Without loss of generality, we can assume L_0 , the initial labor supply to be equal to one so that (2.10) can be written as

$$W = \int_0^\infty e^{-(\delta-n)t} u(c(t))\, dt \qquad (2.12)$$

Mathematically, then, the planning problem can be stated as

$$\left. \begin{array}{l} \underset{\{c(t)\,,\, r(t)\}}{\text{Max}} \quad W = \int_0^\infty e^{-(\delta-n)t} u(c(t))\, dt \\[1em] \text{subject to} \qquad \dot{k} = y - c - (\mu + n)\, k \\[0.5em] \qquad\qquad\qquad \dot{x} = -(r + nx) \\[0.5em] \qquad\qquad\qquad x(0) = x_0 \quad,\quad x(\infty) \geq 0 \\[0.5em] \qquad\qquad\qquad k(0) = k_0 \text{ and } r \geq 0\,,\, c \geq 0 \\[0.5em] \qquad\qquad\qquad\qquad k \geq 0\,,\, x \geq 0\,. \end{array} \right\} \qquad (2.13)$$

Thus, the problem is an optimal control problem with two state variables k and x , and two control variables c and r , with the variables being restricted to be non-negative.

We now proceed to analyze the inter-temporal behavior of the system represented by the above model.

2.2 Optimality Conditions

The necessary conditions for the optimization problem described above can be obtained through the use of Pontryagin's Maximum Principle.[4] The current value Hamiltonian for the problem can be formulated as:

---

[4] See Pontryagin et al. [26], Arrow and Kurz [4], or Shell [34].

14

$$H = u(c) + \lambda_k \{y - c - (\mu + n) k\} + \lambda_x \{ - (r + nx)\} \qquad (2.14)$$

where λ_k and λ_x are the two adjoint variables. According to the Maximum Principle the optimal controls maximize the Hamiltonian at each instant of time. Thus

$$\frac{\partial H}{\partial c} = u'(c) - \lambda_k = 0 \quad \text{if} \quad c > 0$$
$$\leq 0 \quad \text{if} \quad c = 0 \qquad (2.15)$$

$$\frac{\partial H}{\partial r} = \lambda_k \frac{\partial y}{\partial r} - \lambda_x = 0 \quad \text{if} \quad r > 0$$
$$\leq 0 \quad \text{if} \quad r = 0 \qquad (2.16)$$

Additionally the adjoint variable must satisfy the following differential equations:

$$\dot{\lambda}_k = (\delta - n) \lambda_k - \frac{\partial H}{\partial k}$$

or

$$\dot{\lambda}_k = \left[(\mu + \delta) - \frac{\partial y}{\partial k} \right] \lambda_k \qquad (2.17)$$

and

$$\dot{\lambda}_x = (\delta - n) \lambda_x - \frac{\partial H}{\partial x}$$

$$= \delta \lambda_x$$

so that

$$\lambda_x(t) = \lambda_{x,0} e^{\delta t} \qquad (2.18)$$

where $\lambda_{x,0}$ is some positive constant.

Conditions (2.15) to (2.18) are the necessary conditions for optimality of any feasible growth path.

2.3 Economic Interpretation of the Optimality Conditions

The economic interpretation of the optimality conditions is straightforward if we keep in mind that λ_k and λ_x are merely the efficiency prices of the per capita capital and the exhaustible resource

15

respectively, measured in terms of current utility. Thus, according to (2.15), at any time the level of consumption should be set so as to equate its marginal contribution to utility with the efficiency price of the capital: a natural consequence of the assumption that the homogenous output can be used either for consumption or for investment. Similarly (2.16) states that the exhaustible resource should be used at a rate such that its marginal product valued in terms of current utility, is equal to its own efficiency price. These equalities need not hold if the respective controls hit the non-negativity constraints.

Equation (2.17) carries the same interpretation as in traditional neo-classical growth models without exhaustible resource input, i.e., (2.17) can be written as

$$\frac{\partial y}{\partial k} + \frac{\dot{\lambda}_k}{\lambda_k} - \mu - \delta = 0 \quad ,$$

which states that the gross returns from holding a unit of capital (per capita) over a time interval should be equal to the total costs. The gross returns consist of the marginal product $\frac{\partial y}{\partial k}$ plus the capital gains $\frac{\dot{\lambda}_k}{\lambda_k}$. The costs include depreciation μ, and the discount charges δ .[5]

Lastly (2.13) implies that the efficiency price of the exhaustible resource must increase exponentially at the rate of time preference.[6] Stated alternatively, (2.13) implies that the present value of the shadow price of the resource at any time, must remain constant. This stands to reason: if this were not so, then it would be possible to increase the total welfare through re-allocation of the resource stock over time.

---

[5]See, for example, Intriligator [13].

[6]Koopmans' [17] result is an approximate version of this.

16

It is possible to look at the optimality conditions from a slightly different perspective. Using output y as the numeraire, the monetary price of the natural resource is equal to its marginal productivity $\frac{\partial y}{\partial k}$, while the interest rate (the rental price of capital) is equal to the net marginal productivity of capital, $\frac{\partial y}{\partial k} - \mu$. Now from (2.16) the monetary price of the natural resource p is given by

$$p = \frac{\lambda_x}{\lambda_k} \tag{2.19}$$

Defining the net interest rate $\bar{\delta}$ as

$$\delta = \frac{\partial y}{\partial k} - \mu \, ,$$

we have from equation (2.17)

$$\dot{\lambda}_k = (\delta - \bar{\delta}) \, \lambda_k \tag{2.20}$$

Differentiating (2.19) w.r.t. time and then using (2.18) and (2.20), we get

$$\dot{p} = \bar{\delta} \, p \, . \tag{2.21}$$

i.e., the monetary price of the resource, at any instant of time, increases at the prevailing rate of interest. Thus, irrespective of whether one holds one's assets in the form of capital or in the form of the resource, the returns should be the same; for capital assets the returns come from the productivity of the capital while for the resource the returns are provided by the price appreciation. In the context of a decentralized economy, (2.21) implies that for optimality, the monetary flows related

17

to exhaustible resources should be discounted in precisely the same manner as the flows related to capital investments.[7]

We shall now analyze the steady state behavior of the system described above.

2.4 Steady State Equilibria

In view of the finiteness of the resource endowment it is obvious that in steady state the per capita resource usage must go down to zero.[8] Through simple economic argument, it is easy to show that for optimality, the same must be true about the total resource stock X .[9]

With the resource stock exhausted and hence the resource usage rate necessarily fixed at zero, the problem reverts to the standard neo-classical formulation of the optimal growth problem. Thus, it can be shown that if the resource is not indispensable to production (i.e., $y(k,0) > 0$) then there exists a non-trivial steady state solution $(c^{\infty}, k^{\infty}, r^{\infty}, x^{\infty})$ uniquely defined by

---

[7]Equation (2.21) is, in effect, the optimal growth theory analog to Hotelling's [12] condition for inter-temporal optimality of the exhaustible resource usage with exogenous demand specification.
    It should be noted here that the price p , in our formulation as well as in Hotelling's, is net of any extraction costs; it represents the opportunity cost only.

[8]Assuming that the population is non-decreasing, i.e., $n \geq 0$.

[9]E.g., any optimal program with non-zero terminal resource stock can be improved upon by another program which is the same as the previous program except that for some time interval T , the left-over resource stock is also put to use; the resulting additional output being used to augment the current consumption. The superiority of the second program follows from our assumptions of $\frac{\partial y}{\partial r} > 0$ and $u'(c) > 0$.

$$\frac{\partial y}{\partial k} (k^{\infty}, r^{\infty}) = \mu + \delta$$

$$\left. \begin{array}{l} c^{\infty} = y(k^{\infty}, r^{\infty}) - (\mu + n) k^{\infty} \\[6pt] x^{\infty} = r^{\infty} = 0 \end{array} \right\} \qquad (2.22)$$

Alternatively if resource input is essential to production (i.e., $y(k,0) = 0$) then the unique steady state solution would be the trivial solution

$$c^{\infty} = k^{\infty} = r^{\infty} = x^{\infty} = 0 \qquad (2.23)$$

Thus, in either case the long run equilibrium is independent of the initial capital stock k_0 as well as of the resource endowment x_0 , a result very much in the spirit of the similar result in the standard formulation of the optimal growth problem.[10]

Using the strict concavity of u and y , it can be shown that starting from some initially specified (k_0, x_0) , any feasible growth path which satisfies the necessary optimality conditions (2.15) - (2.18) and converges to the appropriate steady state is the unique optimal growth path.[11]

It is appropriate here to address a related issue, i.e., the issue of exhausting the resource in a finite time.

2.5 Optimality of Exhausting the Resource in Finite Time

We noted above that along the optimal path steady state corresponds to the exhaustion of the resource. Thus, the issue relates to

---

[10]See Cass [7], for example.

[11]For a general outline of the proof see Arrow and Kurz [4] or Cass [7].

the determination of the conditions under which the optimal path reaches steady state (with respect to the resource) in infinite time. While it is true that the steady state value of the capital can be approached only asymptotically, the same does not necessarily hold true for the resource. We present below the conditions which ensure that along the optimal path the resource would be exhausted in a finite time. We begin by proving the following lemma about the constant $\lambda_{x,0}$ in equation (2.18).

Lemma: Along any optimal path $\lambda_{x,0} < \infty$.

Proof: Assume to the contrary that for some optimal path $\lambda_{x,0} = \infty$. Then from (2.18), $\lambda_x(t) = \lambda_{x,0} e^{\delta t} = \infty$ for any $t \geq 0$. Accordingly from (2.16) either $r(t) = 0$ at all times or $\lambda_k \frac{\partial y}{\partial r} = \infty$ for some time. If $r(t) = 0$ at all times then $X(\infty) = X(0) > 0$, which as indicated earlier is non-optimal. Hence $\lambda_k \frac{\partial y}{\partial r} = \infty$ for some time. Also since for $r > 0$, $\frac{\partial y}{\partial r} < \infty$ we must have $\lambda_k = \infty$ whenever $r > 0$.

Now from equation (2.17)

$$\frac{\dot{\lambda}_k}{\lambda_k} \leq (\mu + \delta)$$

so that if λ_k is finite at $t = 0$, it can become unbounded only in the infinitely distant future. Thus for the resource to be used at all, λ_k must be infinite at the start. From (2.15), $\lambda_k = \infty \rightarrow c = 0$. If λ_k remains infinite at all times then consumption would always be zero; such a path is obviously non-optimal and hence λ_k must jump to a finite value at some finite time T_*, i.e.,

$$\lambda_k(T_*^-) = \infty \quad \text{and} \quad \lambda_k(T_*^+) = M$$

20

where M is some finite constant.

Integrating (2.17) between T_*^- and T_*^+ we have

$$\ln[\lambda_k(T_*^+)] - \ln[\lambda_k(T_*^-)] = \int_{T_*^-}^{T_*^+} (\mu + \delta - \frac{\partial y}{\partial k})\, dt$$

from which it follow that

$$\int_{T_*^-}^{T_*^+} \frac{\partial y}{\partial k}\, dt = \infty$$

But $\frac{\partial y}{\partial k} \leq \frac{y}{k}$, i.e., the marginal product is lower than the average product.

Hence
$$\int_{T_*^-}^{T_*^+} \frac{y}{k}\, dt \geq \infty$$

Since $k > 0$, the above inequality implies that

$$\int_{T_*^-}^{T_*^+} y\, dt \geq \infty$$

i.e., the total production between T_*^- and T_*^+ must be infinite. This is clearly impossible since finite inputs cannot produce infinite output over an infinitesimally small time interval.

Thus $\lambda_{x,0} = \infty$ leads to solutions which are either non-optimal or infeasible.

Hence $\lambda_{x,0}$ must be finite.

21

Returning to our original problem, let T_e denote the time of exhaustion of the resource i.e., $T_e = \inf\{T : t > T , r(t) = 0\}$ then we can prove the following:

Theorem 1: T_e is arbitrarily large if either

i) $\frac{\partial y}{\partial r}(k,0) = \infty$ or

ii) $y(k,0) = 0$, $u'(0) = \infty$ and $0 \le c \le y$ [12]

Proof: Assume to the contrary that $T_e = T_1$ is the time of exhaustion along some optimal path. Then since for $t > T_1$, $r(t) = 0$ we have from (2.16)

$$\lambda_k \frac{\partial y}{\partial r} \le \lambda_{x,0} \, e^{\delta t} \quad : \quad t > T_1$$

or

$$\frac{\partial y}{\partial r} \le \frac{\lambda_{x,0}}{\lambda_k} e^{\delta t} \quad : \quad t > T_1 \tag{2.24}$$

Now if (i) holds then $\frac{\partial y}{\partial r}(k,0)$ is arbitrarily large. In particular for some $t^* > T_1$

$$\frac{\partial y}{\partial r}(k,0) > \frac{\lambda_{x,0}}{\lambda_k} e^{\delta t^*}$$

as $\lambda_{x,0} < \infty$ and $\lambda_k \ge u'(c) > 0$. However this contradicts (2.24) and hence the first part of the Theorem is proved.

---

[12]This result is similar to the one derived by Vousden [41]; his specifications of the production function and the utility function are considerably more restrictive, however.

Similarly if (ii) holds then since $0 \leq c \leq y(k,0)$ we must have $c = 0$ for $t > T_1$. Accordingly, $\lambda_k \geq u'(0) = \infty$ i.e., λ_k would be arbitrarily large for $t > T_1$. Therefore, for some $t^* > T_1$

$$\lambda_k \geq \frac{\lambda_{x,0}}{\frac{\partial y}{\partial r}} e^{\delta t}$$

Once again we contradict (2.24) and this proves the second part of the Theorem.

Conversely we can prove the following:

Theorem 2: The optimal time of exhaustion T_e is arbitrarily large only if either

i) $\frac{\partial y}{\partial r} (k,0) = \infty$, or

ii) $y(k,0) = 0$

Proof: If $T_e = \infty$ then (2.16) holds as an equality for any arbitrarily large t i.e.,

$$\lambda_k \frac{\partial y}{\partial r} = \lambda_{x,0} e^{\delta t} \qquad (2.25)$$

The R.H.S. of (2.25) however goes to ∞ as t gets arbitrarily large. Thus either λ_k or $\frac{\partial y}{\partial r}$ must get arbitrarily large as $r \to 0$ for large t.

For $\lambda_k = \infty$ it is necessary to have $c = 0$. If $y(k,0)$ were to be greater than zero then we would have a situation where as r approaches zero, output y gets used solely for investment without the prospect of any subsequent consumption. Such a program would be obviously non-optimal. Accordingly for $\lambda_k \to \infty$ we must have $y(k,0) = 0$.

23

Alternatively if $\lambda_k < \infty$ then we must have $\frac{\partial y}{\partial r}(k,0) = \infty$. And hence the Theorem is established.

Thus the assumptions about the role of the natural resources in the production function play a crucial role in deciding whether the natural resources should be used over a finite time or made to last indefinitely.

The conclusions above closely relate to some of the existing controversy regarding the use of exhaustible raw materials. As we noted previously in Chapter I one of the dominant themes in the conservationist writing is the concern that the current usage trends in natural resources would cause their depletion some time in the future. Underlying this concern is the belief that the resources should be consumed at such a rate that they would last indefinitely. The result proved above would indicate that even in our static technology model with no recycling possibilities it is optimal to use up the resources in a finite time unless either their marginal product is unbounded or they are essential to production. To the extent that the decision to exhaust the resources over a finite time depends upon their role in the production process, an empirical study of their role should be enlightening in discussions of some of the conservationist controversies.

For the rest of this study we shall assume that the production function is of Cobb-Douglas type. Among other things this assumption implies that

$$\lim_{r \to 0} y(k,r) = 0$$

and

$$\lim_{r \to 0} \frac{\partial y}{\partial r}(k,r) = \infty$$

$\qquad\qquad (2.26)$

24

i.e., the resources are essential to production and their marginal product becomes unbounded as the usage rate approaches zero.

A few words of explanation are in order for this assumption. Firstly it is thought that the results would be more relevant to the current controversy were we to assume that the resources are essential to production-- for, after all, this is the main thrust of the conservationist argument.

Secondly there is the consideration that the case where resources are not essential to production is much less interesting analytically; the long run behaviour of the economy, in that case, degenerates to that obtained in the traditional formulation of the optimal growth problem.

Finally and perhaps most importantly the log-linear character of Cobb-Douglas technology permits a level of analysis which would be impossible for the more general production functions. Hopefully, the insights gained from this analysis will be of use for future analysis with more general production functions.

We shall turn now to a detailed analysis of the optimal growth trajectories. As we shall see in the next chapter, the optimal growth paths in the present formulation have several interesting characteristics which set them apart from the paths obtained for the standard neo-classical growth models. We shall show, for example, that the monotonic convergence of the optimal growth paths to the steady state, typical of neo-classical models, need not be true in the present framework. In particular we shall show that there exist optimal paths along which capital and consumption are increased for some time, only to be decreased to the steady state subsequently.

25

CHAPTER III

OPTIMAL GROWTH PATHS FOR COBB-DOUGLAS TECHNOLOGIES

In this chapter we present a detailed analysis of the optimal growth paths assuming that the production technology is described by a constant returns to scale, Cobb-Douglas production function. In Section 3.1 we assume the technology to be static. In Section 3.2 we extend the analysis to include technical progress. Section 3.3 provides a summary of the main results.

3.1 Cobb-Douglas Technology, No Technical Progress

3.1.1 Preliminaries

Assume that the production function is of Cobb-Douglas type i.e.,

$$Y = A_0 \, K^\alpha \, R^\beta \, L^{1-\alpha-\beta} \tag{3.1}$$

where A_0, α and β are positive constants such that $\alpha + \beta < 1$. Without loss of generality A_0 can be assumed equal to one and then in per capita terms (3.1) can be expressed as

$$y = k^\alpha \, r^\beta \tag{3.2}$$

Among other things (3.2) implies that

$$\left.\begin{array}{l} y(k,0) = 0 \\[1em] \dfrac{\partial y}{\partial r}(k,0) = \infty \end{array}\right\} \tag{3.3}$$

and

26

Thus the resource input is essential to production and accordingly, as noted in the previous chapter, the only steady state possible is the null state

$$c^\infty = k^\infty = r^\infty = x^\infty = 0 \qquad (3.4)$$

Furthermore the unboundedness of $\frac{\partial y}{\partial r}$ $(k,0)$ implies that the steady state would be approached asymptotically, since optimally the resource stock cannot be exhausted in a finite time.

Assume also that the elasticity of marginal utility of consumption $\sigma = -c \frac{u''(c)}{u'(c)} > 0$ is constant so that the utility function is of the type[1]

$$u(c) = \frac{1}{1-\sigma} c^{1-\sigma} \qquad (3.5)$$

Notice that for the assumed $u(\cdot)$

$$u'(0) = \infty \qquad (3.6)$$

The Optimality Conditions

(3.3) and (3.6) ensure that the optimal solution would be an interior point solution and accordingly the optimality conditions (2.15) and (2.16) are reduced to

$$u'(c) = \lambda_k \qquad (3.7)$$

and

$$\lambda_k \frac{\partial y}{\partial r} = \lambda_x \qquad (3.7)$$

---

[1]For $\sigma = 1$, however, the utility function would be logarithmic i.e., $u(c) = \ln c$.

Differentiating (3.7) w.r.t. time

$$u''(c) \, \dot{c} = \dot{\lambda}_k$$

so that
$$\dot{\lambda}_k / \lambda_k = \frac{u''(c)}{u'(c)} \, \dot{c} = -\sigma \cdot \frac{\dot{c}}{c} \tag{3.9}$$

Combining (2.17) with (3.9) and using (3.2) we get

$$\sigma \, \dot{c}/c = \alpha \, k^{\alpha-1} \, r^\beta - (\mu+\delta) \tag{3.10}$$

Next substituting from (3.7) into (3.8)

$$u'(c) \, \frac{\partial y}{\partial r} = \lambda_x$$

Again differentiating w.r.t. time

$$u''(c) \, \dot{c} \, \frac{\partial y}{\partial r} + u'(c) \left[\frac{\partial^2 y}{\partial r^2} \, \dot{r} + \frac{\partial^2 y}{\partial k \, \partial r} \, \dot{k} \right] = \dot{\lambda}_x = \delta\lambda_x$$

or
$$u'(c) \left[\frac{\partial y}{\partial r} \, \frac{u''(c)}{u'(c)} \, \dot{c} + \frac{\partial^2 y}{\partial r^2} \, \dot{r} + \frac{\partial^2 y}{\partial k \, \partial r} \, \dot{k} \right] = \delta \, u'(c) \, \frac{\partial y}{\partial r}$$

or
$$-\sigma \, \frac{\partial y}{\partial r} \, \frac{\dot{c}}{c} + \frac{\partial^2 y}{\partial r^2} \, \dot{r} + \frac{\partial^2 y}{\partial k \, \partial r} \, \dot{k} = \delta \, \frac{\partial y}{\partial r} \,. \tag{3.11}$$

Now using (3.2) we get

$$-\sigma \, \frac{\dot{c}}{c} \, \beta \, k^\alpha \, r^{\beta-1} + \beta(\beta-1) \, k^\alpha \, r^{\beta-2} \, \dot{r} + \alpha\beta \, k^{\alpha-1} \, r^{\beta-1} \, \dot{k} = \delta\beta \, k^\alpha \, r^{\beta-1}$$

or
$$-\sigma \, \frac{\dot{c}}{c} + (\beta-1) \, \frac{\dot{r}}{r} + \alpha \, \frac{\dot{k}}{k} = \delta \,. \tag{3.12}$$

28

Thus, any optimal trajectory must satisfy the following set of differential equations:

$$\frac{\dot{k}}{k} = k^{\alpha-1} r^\beta - (\mu+n) - \frac{c}{k} \qquad \text{(a)}$$

$$\frac{\dot{x}}{x} = - (\frac{r}{x} + n) \qquad \text{(b)}$$

$$\frac{\dot{c}}{c} = \frac{1}{\sigma} [\alpha k^{\alpha-1} r^\beta - (\mu+\delta)] \qquad \text{(c)}$$

$$\frac{\dot{r}}{r} = \frac{1}{1-\beta} \left[\alpha \frac{\dot{k}}{k} - \sigma \frac{\dot{c}}{c} - \delta \right] \qquad \text{(d)}$$

(3.13)

where the first two equations merely describe the behavior of the state variables for the Cobb-Douglas production function (cf. eq. (2.7)).

The system of equations (3.13) is non-linear. In general, such a system would be extremely difficult to analyze. However, because of its special structure, (3.13) admits of a simple linear solution provided the initial endowments of the capital and the resource are related to each other in a certain way. In fact we show below that there exists a unique monotonically increasing function $g(\cdot)$ such that if the initial endowments k_0 and x_0 satisfy

$$x_0 = g(k_0) , \qquad (3.14)$$

then the system has a linear solution. For reasons to be elaborated below, we shall term endowments satisfying (3.14) to be the balanced endowments of capital and the exhaustible resource.

3.1.2 Optimal Trajectories from Balanced Endowments

Assume that

$$k = k_* \, e^{\gamma_k t}$$

$$x = x_* \, e^{\gamma_x t}$$

$$\left. \right\} \qquad (3.15)$$

$$c = c_* \, e^{\gamma_c t}$$

and $$r = r_* \, e^{\gamma_r t}$$

is a solution to (3.13), where $k_* \ldots r_*$ and $\gamma_k \ldots \gamma_r$ are constants. Substituting from (3.15) into (3.13) we get

$$\gamma_k = (k_* \, e^{\gamma_k t})^{\alpha-1} \, (r_* \, e^{\gamma_r t})^{\beta} - (\mu+n) - \frac{c_*}{k_*} \, e^{(\gamma_c - \gamma_k)t} \qquad (3.16)$$

$$\gamma_x = -\frac{r_*}{x_*} \, e^{(\gamma_r - \gamma_x)t} - n \qquad (3.17)$$

$$\gamma_c = \frac{1}{\sigma} \, [\alpha(k_* e^{\gamma_k t})^{\alpha-1} \, (r_* \, e^{\gamma_r t})^{\beta} - (\mu+\delta)] \qquad (3.18)$$

$$\gamma_r = \frac{1}{1-\beta} \, [\alpha\gamma_k - \sigma\gamma_c - \delta] \qquad (3.19)$$

These four relations should be identically true at all times for (3.15) to be a solution to (3.13). Accordingly we get the following conditions:

From (3.18) $$e^{[\gamma_k(\alpha-1) + \gamma_r\beta]t} = \text{const.}$$

So that $$\gamma_k(\alpha-1) + \gamma_r\beta = 0$$

or $$\gamma_k = (\frac{\beta}{1-\alpha}) \cdot \gamma_r \qquad (3.20)$$

Then from (3.20) and (3.16) we get

$$Y_c = Y_k \qquad (3.21)$$

Also from (3.19), (3.20) and (3.21) we get

$$\frac{1-\alpha}{\beta} Y_c = \frac{1}{1-\beta} [(\alpha-\sigma) Y_c - \delta]$$

or $$(\frac{1-\alpha}{\beta} - \frac{\alpha-\sigma}{1-\beta})Y_c = - \frac{\delta}{1-\beta}$$

or $$\frac{1-\alpha-\beta+\sigma\beta}{\beta} Y_c = - \delta$$

Thus $$Y_k = Y_c = - \frac{\delta\beta}{(1-\alpha-\beta+\sigma\beta)} \qquad (3.22)$$

Lastly from (3.18) we must have

$$Y_r = Y_x \qquad (3.23)$$

Combining this with (3.20) and (3.22) we get

$$Y_r = Y_x = - \frac{(1-\alpha)\delta}{(1-\alpha-\beta+\sigma\beta)} \qquad (3.24)$$

Thus the four rate constants Y_c, Y_k, Y_r and Y_x are completely determined by the technology parameters α and β and the taste parameters σ and δ, through (3.22) and (3.24). Notice that for all permissible values of α, β, σ and δ, all the 'gammas' would be negative.

Using (3.22) and (3.24), equations (3.16)-(3.18) can be simplified to

31

$$\gamma_k = k_*^{\alpha-1}\, r_*^{\beta} - (\mu+n) - \frac{c_*}{k_*} \tag{3.25}$$

$$\gamma_x = - (\frac{r_*}{x_*} + n) \tag{3.26}$$

and

$$\gamma_k = \frac{1}{\sigma}\, [\alpha\, k_*^{\alpha-1}\, r_*^{\beta} - (\mu+\delta)] \tag{3.27}$$

From (3.27)

$$r_* = \left[\frac{\sigma\gamma_k + (\mu+\delta)}{\alpha}\right]^{\frac{1}{\beta}} \cdot k_*^{\frac{1-\alpha}{\beta}} \quad, \tag{3.28}$$

then from (3.25) and (3.28)

$$c_* = \left[\frac{(\sigma-\alpha)\,\gamma_k + (\mu+\delta)}{\alpha} - (\mu+n)\right] k_* \tag{3.29}$$

Also from (3.26)

$$r_* = -(\gamma_x + n)\, x_*^{2} \tag{3.30}$$

  Thus we have three independent relations, among the four constants k_*, x_*, c_* and r_*, which are necessary for (3.15) to be a

---

[2]Notice that unless $n < -\gamma_x$, equation (3.30) would be absurd as neither r_* nor x_* can be negative. Thus, we must have

$$\frac{\delta\,(1-\alpha)}{(1-\alpha-\beta+\sigma\beta)} > n$$

or $\delta > \frac{n\,(1-\alpha-\beta+\sigma\beta)}{(1-\alpha)}$. (cf. footnote 3, Chapter II) It can be shown that with δ so constrained, the constants in (3.28) and (3.29) would also be positive, keeping those relations meaningful. The constraint on δ would also ensure the convergence of the welfare functional.
  I have not proved it but I suspect that the solution would also exist for the limiting case $\delta = \frac{n(1-\alpha-\beta+\sigma\beta)}{1-\alpha}$. However, in that case some further restrictions may be necessary on the values of the various parameters.

solution to (3.13). In general, for an arbitrarily specified k_0 and x_0, it would be impossible to satisfy these relationships simultaneously. However, if k_0 and x_0 were such that

$$x_0 = \frac{1}{[-(\gamma_x + n)]} \cdot \left[\frac{\sigma \gamma_k + (\mu + \delta)}{\alpha} \right]^{\frac{1}{\beta}} \cdot k_0^{\frac{1-\alpha}{\beta}} \qquad (3.31)$$

then the three relations (3.28)-(3.30) could be satisfied and accordingly (3.15) would be a solution to (3.13). Furthermore, the negativity of the 'gammas' ensures that along the postulated solution everything-- resource, capital and consumption-- exponentially decays to zero. This, as indicated previously, is the steady state for the system. Thus, if the initial endowments satisfy (3.31) then the postulated solution would indeed represent the unique optimal growth path; the constants c_* and r_* , determined from (3.28)-(3.30) for (k_0 , x_0) , being the optimal initial controls c_0 and r_0 , respectively.

Notice that in (3.31) x_0 is a monotonically increasing, unique function of k_0 .

Using (3.22) and (3.24), it can be shown that along the optimal path, at any time, $k(t) = k_0 e^{\gamma_k t}$ and $x(t) = x_0 e^{\gamma_x t}$ still satisfy (3.31). Thus, once the economy attains endowments satisfying (3.31), it will preserve that relationship forever. It is precisely for this reason that we term the endowments satisfying (3.31) to be the balanced endowments. Starting with a balanced endowment, the optimal approach to the steady state involves nothing more than tracing the locus of (3.31) from (k_0 , x_0) to the origin.

A few more observations regarding the optimal paths from the balanced endowments are in order here. First, notice that along the

33

optimal path

$$\frac{\dot{y}}{y} = \alpha \frac{\dot{k}}{k} + \beta \frac{\dot{r}}{r} = \alpha \gamma_k + \beta \gamma_r = \gamma_k \quad . \tag{3.32}$$

Thus, capital, consumption and the output all decline at the same exponential rate γ_k; we can consider this rate to be the 'natural growth
rate' of the economy.

Secondly, along the optimal path the savings ratio $s = 1 - \frac{c}{y}$
remains constant and can be shown to be

$$s = \frac{\alpha(\gamma_k + \mu + n)}{\sigma\gamma_k + \mu + \delta} \tag{3.33}$$

This is not too different from the optimal steady state savings ratio of
$\bar{s} = \frac{\alpha(\mu + n)}{\mu + \delta}$, obtained for the traditional neo-classical growth models.[3]

The monetary interest rate $\bar{\delta}$, mentioned in the last chapter,
also remains constant and is smaller than δ, the time preference rate
for the utility of consumption. In fact, it can be shown that

$$\bar{\delta} = \frac{\partial y}{\partial k} - \mu = \delta + \sigma\gamma_k = \frac{\delta(1-\alpha-\beta)}{(1-\alpha-\beta+\sigma\beta)} < \delta \tag{3.34}$$

The last observation relates to the fact that so far we implic-
itly assumed the capital investments to be reversible. The assumption
would be irrelevant so long as the desired rate of disinvestment, γ_k,

---

[3]See for example, Shell [33].

[4]As we shall see later on, the presence of technical progress can
cause a reversal of this inequality.

does not exceed the rate of capital attrition through depreciation and population growth, $(\mu+n)$; i.e., as long as

$$|\gamma_k| = \frac{\delta\beta}{1-\alpha-\beta+\sigma\beta} < (\mu+n)$$

Notice that the above inequality would be valid for almost any realistic set of values for δ, σ, α, β and μ . Accordingly, we need not be overly concerned with the reversibility assumption.

Having thus fully analyzed the optimal behavior for the balanced endowments, the obvious question now is: What happens if the arbitrarily specified k_0 and x_0 do not satisfy (3.31), as would be the case in general? Does the postulated linear solution (3.15) still have any meaning in that case? In fact, it does. We show below that the optimal path, starting from any unbalanced endowment, is such that it tries to reduce the original imbalance and gradually approaches a path which would have resulted, had it started with a balanced endowment initially. How-ever, we first present a numerical example to illustrate the optimal behavior from balanced endowments.

3.1.3 A Numerical Example

Let $\qquad$ $\alpha = 0.25$

$\qquad\qquad\qquad\quad \beta = 0.05$

$\qquad\qquad\qquad\quad \mu = 0.05$

$\qquad\qquad\qquad\quad \delta = 0.03$

$\qquad\qquad\qquad\quad n = 0.02$

and $\qquad\qquad\quad \sigma = 1.0$

be the values of the basic parameters of the model.[5] Then the balanced endowments satisfy

$$x_\star = 7.63 \times 10^{-9} \cdot k_\star^{15}$$

For an optimal path starting from some balanced endowment we would have

$$c_\star = 0.244 \; k_\star$$
$$r_\star = 0.01 \; x_\star$$
$$\gamma_k = \gamma_c = -.002$$

and
$$\gamma_x = \gamma_r = -.03$$

The above example is unrealistic in that it assumes completely static technology. However, assuming that the values of the parameters used in this example are roughly correct, there are several noteworthy aspects of the above results:

i) Along the balanced endowment path, $x_\star$ is highly sensitive to changes in $k_\star$. A 1% change in $k_\star$ causes a 15% change in $x_\star$. The sensitivity would have been even higher, had we used a lower value for β . The high sensitivity suggests an interesting hypothesis for empirical research; namely, could it be that the current concern about the growing scarcity of natural resources stems not from any absolute decline in the known reserves of the exhaustible resources, but from the failure to replenish the resource reserve (through new discoveries etc.) at such a rate as to keep balance with the rapidly increasing capital stock.

---

[5] To my knowledge no esimates exist for the value of β . Thus while the assumed values of the other parameters are thought to be fairly representative, the assumed value of β is nothing more than speculation.

ii) Even though eventually everything decays to zero, the depletion of the resources even in this static technology model is much faster
than the decline in either the capital or the consumption. Along the
optimal path, for example, capital and consumption would be halved about
every 350 years while the resource stock and the usage rate would be
halved about every 23 years.

iii) The optimal resource reserves at any time represent about
100 years of resource consumption at the current usage rate. For comparison, Limits to Growth [20] assumes the global reserves to be equal to 250
years' supply, at the current usage rates.

iv) The monetary interest rate $\bar{\delta}$ would be equal to .028
compared to a value of 0.03 for the rate for discounting utilities.

v) The savings rate $s \approx 0.219$, is practically the same as
the optimal steady state savings rate in the conventional formulation with
$\beta=0$.

vi) Lastly notice that for the existence of balanced endow-
ments, the rate of population growth must not exceed $|\gamma_x| = .03$.

The existence of technical progress as well as any imbalance
in the initial endowment will, of course, modify some of the above conclusions. We shall return to this example, at appropriate times, to
see their influence.

3.1.4 Optimal Trajectories from Arbitrary Endowments

Let the optimal trajectory corresponding to an arbitrarily
specified initial condition (k_0 , x_0) be given by

37

$$k(t) = k_* e^{\gamma_k t} k_1(t)$$

$$x(t) = x_* e^{\gamma_x t} x_1(t)$$

$$c(t) = c_* e^{\gamma_c t} c_1(t)$$

$$r(t) = r_* e^{\gamma_r t} r_1(t)$$

(3.35)

where the constants $k_* \ldots r_*$ and $\gamma_k \ldots \gamma_r$ satisfy (3.22), (3.24) and (3.28)-(3.30) and c_1, k_1, r_1, and x_1 are some yet unspecified functions of time chosen so that

$$k_0 = k_* \cdot k_1(0)$$

and

$$x_0 = x_* \cdot x_1(0)$$

(3.36)

i.e., the arbitrarily specified initial condition is satisfied. Notice that c_1, k_1, r_1 and x_1 can be respectively considered as normalized consumption, capital, resource usage rate and the resource stock; the normalizing factors being the corresponding quantities along some 'balanced capital-resource endowment.' Using (3.34), equations (3.13) can be expressed in terms of the new variables, e.g.

$$\gamma_k + \frac{\dot{k}_1}{k_1} = (k_*^{\alpha-1} \, r_*^{\beta})(k_1^{\alpha-1} \, r_1^{\beta}) \; (e^{\gamma_k t})^{\alpha-1} \, (e^{\gamma_r t})^{\beta} -$$

$$(\mu+n) - \frac{c_*}{k_*} \cdot \frac{c_1}{k_1} e^{(\gamma_c - \gamma_k)t}$$

$$\gamma_x + \frac{\dot{x}_1}{x_1} = - \left[\frac{r_*}{x_*} \frac{r_1}{x_1} \cdot e^{(\gamma_r - \gamma_x)t} + n \right]$$

$$\gamma_c + \frac{\dot{c}_1}{c_1} = \frac{1}{\sigma}\left[\alpha(k_*^{\alpha-1}\ r_*^{\beta})\ (k_1^{\alpha-1}\ r_1^{\beta})\ (e^{\gamma_k t})^{\alpha-1}\ (e^{\gamma_k t})^{\beta} - (\mu + \delta)\right]$$

$$\gamma_r + \frac{\dot{r}_1}{r_1} = \frac{1}{1-\beta}\left[\alpha(\gamma_k + \frac{\dot{k}_1}{k_1}) - \sigma(\gamma_c + \frac{\dot{c}_1}{c_1}) - \delta\right]$$

Using (3.22), (3.24) and (3.28)-(3.30), and after some rearrangement, we get

$$\frac{\dot{k}_1}{k_1} = \frac{1}{\alpha}\left[(1-\beta)\ \frac{\dot{r}_1}{r_1} + \sigma\frac{\dot{c}_1}{c_1}\right] \qquad \text{(a)}$$

$$\frac{\dot{x}_1}{x_1} = (\gamma_x + n)\left[\frac{r_1}{x_1} - 1\right] \qquad \text{(b)}$$

$$\frac{\dot{c}_1}{c_1} = \frac{\sigma\gamma_k + (\mu+\delta)}{\sigma}\left[k_1^{\alpha-1}\ r_1^{\beta} - 1\right] \qquad \text{(c)}$$

(3.37)

and

$$\frac{\dot{r}_1}{r_1} = \frac{\alpha}{1-\beta}\ \frac{c_*}{k_*}\left[1 - \frac{c_1}{k_1}\right] \qquad \text{(d)}$$

Consider the steady state of (3.37). In steady state we have

$$\frac{\dot{k}_1}{k_1} = \frac{\dot{c}_1}{c_1} = \frac{\dot{r}_1}{r_1} = \frac{\dot{x}_1}{x_1} = 0$$

so that the steady state is given by

$$c_1^{\infty} = k_1^{\infty}$$

$$r_1^{\infty} = x_1^{\infty}$$

$$(r_1^{\infty}) = (k_1^{\infty})^{\frac{1-\alpha}{\beta}}$$

(3.33)

39

Thus in the steady state all four variables must be less than one, equal to one or greater than one.

Notice that the growth trajectories obtained by combining the above steady state solution with the exponentially decaying solution for the balanced endowment conditions i.e., the trajectories:

$$
\left.
\begin{aligned}
k(t) &= k_* k_1^\infty \, e^{\gamma_k t} \\[1em]
x(t) &= x_* x_1^\infty \, e^{\gamma_x t} \\[1em]
c(t) &= c_* c_1^\infty \, e^{\gamma_c t} \\[1em]
r(t) &= r_* r_1^\infty \, e^{\gamma_r t}
\end{aligned}
\right\} \tag{3.39}
$$

and

are such that the new constants $c_* c_1^\infty$, $k_* k_1^\infty$, $r_* r_1^\infty$, and $x_* x_1^\infty$ again satisfy the relations (3.28)-(3.30). Thus, when (3.37) approaches steady state, (3.35) behaves as if it had started on the balanced endowment locus with initial endowments $k_* k_1^\infty$ and $x_* x_1^\infty$ instead of k_0 and x_0 .

Notice further that if we were to obtain a solution of (3.35) by choosing c_1 , k_1 , r_1 and x_1 such that the normalized variables converged to the steady state (3.38), then the original variables would converge to the null steady state (3.4). But any solution of (3.13) which, starting from the initially specified endowments, converges to the steady state (3.4), is the unique optimal growth path. Accordingly, the problem of finding the optimal growth path is reduced to finding a solution of (3.37) which, starting from the arbitrarily specified $(k_1(0), x_1(0))$ converges to the steady state (3.38).

40

We show below that corresponding to any arbitrarily given $(k_1(0)$, $x_1(0))$, there is a unique solution of (3.37) which converges to the steady state (3.38).

Analysis of the Normalized System

(3.37a) can be directly integrated to yield

$$k_1 = J \; r_1^{\frac{1-\beta}{\alpha}} \; c_1^{\frac{\sigma}{\alpha}} \tag{3.40}$$

where J is an arbitrary positive constant, determined by $k_1(0)$ and $x_1(0)$. Equation (3.40) can be used to eliminate k_1 from (3.37c) and (3.37d) e.g.,

$$\frac{\dot{c_1}}{c_1} = \frac{\sigma \gamma_k + (\mu + \delta)}{\sigma} \left[J^{\alpha-1} \cdot r_1^{\frac{-(1-\alpha-\beta)}{\alpha}} \cdot c_1^{\frac{\sigma(\alpha-1)}{\alpha}} - 1 \right] \tag{3.41}$$

and

$$\frac{\dot{r_1}}{r_1} = \frac{\alpha}{1-\beta} \frac{c_*}{k_*} \left[1 - \frac{c_1^{(1-\sigma/\alpha)} \cdot r_1^{\frac{-(1-\beta)}{\alpha}}}{J} \right] \tag{3.42}$$

The system of equations (3.37b), (3.40)-(3.42) is equivalent to (3.37). Notice that (3.41) and (3.42) are expressed in terms of c_1 and r_1 only, and accordingly can be analyzed independently of (3.37b) and (3.40). Depending upon whether $\sigma > = < \alpha$, we have three cases to analyze. The case where $\sigma = \alpha$ is the easiest to analyze and will be treated before the other two.

41

Case I: $\sigma = \alpha$

In this case (3.41) and (3.42) are decoupled and (3.42) reduces to

$$\frac{\dot{r}_1}{r_1} = \frac{\alpha}{1-\beta} \frac{c_*}{k_*} \left[1 - \frac{r_1^{\frac{-(1-\beta)}{\alpha}}}{J} \right] \qquad (3.43)$$

with only one variable r_1.

The steady state of (3.43) is given by

$$\frac{\dot{r}_1}{r_1} = 0 \rightarrow r_1^\infty = J^{-\frac{\alpha}{1-\beta}} \qquad (3.44)$$

It is easy to see that (3.43) represents an unstable system and the steady state will be realized only if r_1 is constrained to the steady state at all times. Thus the only stable solution of (3.43) is

$$r_1(t) = J^{\frac{-\alpha}{1-\beta}} \qquad (3.45)$$

Now substituting from (3.45) into (3.41) we get

$$\frac{\dot{c}_1}{c_1} = \frac{\alpha \gamma_k + (\mu+\delta)}{\alpha} \left[J^{-\frac{\alpha\beta}{1-\beta}} c_1^{(\alpha-1)} - 1 \right] \qquad (3.46)$$

At the steady state

$$c_1^\infty = J^{-\frac{\alpha\beta}{(1-\beta)(1-\alpha)}} \qquad (3.47)$$

42

Unlike (3.43), equation (3.46) is stable and c_1 approaches steady state from any $c_1(0)$.

By substituting (3.45) into (3.37b), it can be easily seen that the only stable solution to (3.37b) is

$$x_1(t) = r_1(t) = J^{-\frac{\alpha}{1-\beta}} \qquad (3.48)$$

Lastly substituting (3.45) into (3.40) we have

$$k_1(t) = c_1(t) \quad . \qquad (3.49)$$

Thus for an arbitrary pair $(k_1(0)$, $x_1(0))$, choosing $r_1(0) = x_1(0)$ and $c_1(0) = k_1(0)$, will move the system towards the steady state in a unique fashion. We have already shown however that any path starting from the initial specifications, satisfying the necessary conditions, and converging to the steady state is the unique optimal path. Accordingly the solution just described is the unique optimal growth path. Figure 3.1 shows typical optimal trajectories for 'capital-poor', 'capital-rich' and 'balanced endowment' economies, in terms of the normalized variables.

Let us pause briefly to elaborate on the above result. Notice that through an appropriate choice of $(k_*$, $x_*)$ any given $(k_0$, $x_0)$ can be reduced to $(k_1(0), 1)$(i.e., choose $x_* = x_0$). $k_1(0)$ is then a measure of the abundance of capital relative to the exhaustible resource; if $k_1(0) < 1$ then the economy is relatively better endowed with the resource and vice versa. The previous analysis shows that along the optimal path, the economy changes its relative consumption in proportion

43

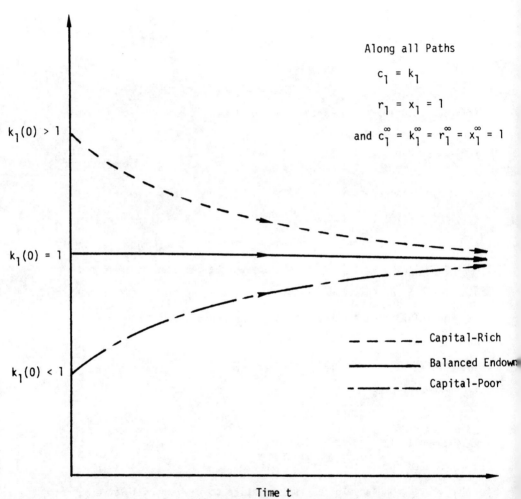

Figure 3.1: Typical Optimal Trajectories for $\sigma = \alpha$:
Normalized Variables

44

to the relative capital endowment. Notice that the overall effect of
this proportional change is eventually to end the imbalance. The increased
consumption in the capital-rich case exceeds the incremental output due
to the additional capital stock, resulting in a gradual decapitalization
and hence reduction of the original imbalance. Just the opposite happens
in case of relative capital scarcity; consumption is curtailed not only
to compensate for the reduced output but also to cummulate more capital,
thus, once again eliminating the imbalance, eventually.

It is possible to look at the problem from another perspective,
i.e., from the resource side. A relative capital scarcity, by definition,
is same as a relative abundance of natural resources. The optimal solution from this viewpoint involves increased resource use to build capital
stock at a faster pace, to eventually bring it into conformity with the
more generous resource endowment.

Irrespective of the initial capital stock, the optimal path
eventually behaves as if it had started with the balanced endowment corresponding to the initial resource stock. Thus the behavior of the
optimal growth path, in the long run, is controlled only by the initial
resource endowment; the initial capital stock determines only the transient
condition of 'starvation' or 'feast' in the early periods.

Non-Monotonicity of the Growth Path

An interesting characteristic of the optimal growth path is
the fact that, unlike in the traditional neo-classical formulations,
capital and consumption do not have to converge to the steady state,
monotonically. Specifically it is possible now that along an optimal
path a capital-poor economy will increase its capital and consumption for

45

a while, only to decrease them subsequently. For this to happen it is necessary only that for some time interval T

$$\frac{\dot{c}_1}{c_1} \geq |\gamma_k|$$

so that

$$\frac{\dot{c}}{c} = \gamma_k + \frac{\dot{c}_1}{c_1} \geq 0$$

From (3.46) it is clear that this will happen when

$$\frac{\alpha\gamma_k + (\mu+\delta)}{\alpha} \; [c_1^{\alpha-1} - 1] \geq - \gamma_k \qquad 6$$

i.e., when

$$c_1 \leq \left[\frac{\alpha\gamma_k + (\mu+\delta)}{(\mu+\delta)} \right]^{\frac{1}{1-\alpha}} \qquad (3.50)$$

Since along the optimal path $c_1 = k_1$, the optimal path will necessarily have a segment along which capital and consumption are increased provided

$$k_1(0) < \left[\frac{\alpha\gamma_k + (\mu+\delta)}{\mu+\delta} \right]^{\frac{1}{1-\alpha}} \qquad (3.51)$$

The increase will continue until the inequality sign in (3.51) is reversed through capital accumulation. Observe that because of the negativity of γ_k , the RHS of (3.51) must necessarily be less than one; typically, however, it will be close to one.

---

[6] Notice that for $r_1(0) = x_1(0) = 1$, the constant $J = 1$ (c.f. eq. (3.45)).

It should be noted that along the optimal path the other possibility, i.e., decreasing consumption and capital followed by increasing segments, is not possible. Thus, once the downfall starts, it is downhill all the way!

Figure 3.2 shows the typical optimal trajectories for capital stock for 'capital-rich', 'capital-poor' and 'balanced endowment' economies. The 'capital-poor' economy is assumed to be in accordance with (3.51).

Cases II and III: $\sigma \neq \alpha$

We now turn to the somewhat more complicated cases corresponding to $\sigma < \alpha$ and $\sigma > \alpha$. Unlike in the case for $\sigma = \alpha$, now equations (3.41) and (3.42) cannot be decoupled and must be analyzed simultaneously. While the analysis does tend to be a little involved at places, the underlying approach is rather simple. Through phase diagrams in (r_1, c_1) plane and (r_1, x_1) plane we shall try to characterize the paths which, starting from the arbitrarily specified $(k_1(0), x_1(0))$ converge to the steady state (3.38).

We begin by a description of the phase diagram in (r_1, c_1) plane, corresponding to equations (3.41) and (3.42). From (3.41) at $\dot{c}_1 = 0$

$$r_1^{\frac{-(1-\alpha-\beta)}{\alpha}} \cdot c_1^{\frac{\sigma(\alpha-1)}{\alpha}} = J^{1-\alpha}$$

Along $\dot{c}_1 = 0$

$$\left. \frac{dc_1}{dr_1} \right|_{\dot{c}_1 = 0} = -\frac{1-\alpha-\beta}{\sigma(1-\alpha)} \frac{c_1}{r_1} < 0 \qquad (3.52)$$

47

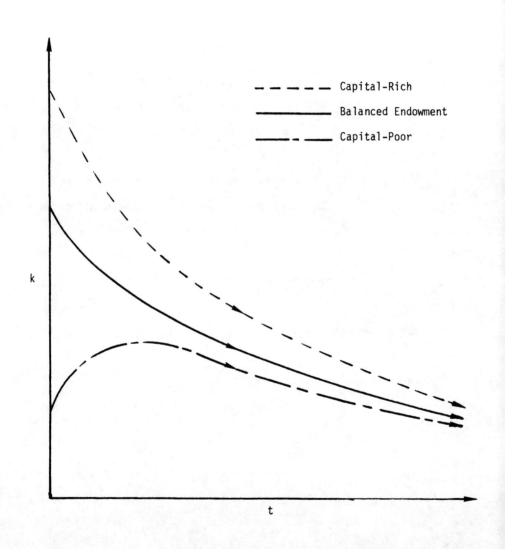

Figure 3.2: Typical Optimal Trajectories for Capital Stock for $\delta = \alpha$

48

and
$$\left.\frac{d^2 c_1}{dr_1^2}\right|_{\dot{c}_1 = 0} = \frac{1-\alpha-\beta}{(1-\alpha)} \cdot \frac{c_1}{r_1^2} \cdot [\frac{1-\alpha-\beta}{\sigma(1-\alpha)} + 1] > 0 \qquad (3.53)$$

Also from (3.42), at $\dot{r}_1 = 0$

$$c_1^{1-\sigma/\alpha} \cdot r_1^{\frac{-(1-\beta)}{\alpha}} = J$$

Along $\dot{r}_1 = 0$

$$\left.\frac{dc_1}{dr_1}\right|_{\dot{r}_1 = 0} = - \frac{(1-\beta)}{\sigma-\alpha} \frac{c_1}{r_1} \begin{array}{l} < 0 \quad \text{if} \quad \sigma > \alpha \\ > 0 \quad \text{if} \quad \sigma < \alpha \end{array} \qquad (3.54)$$

$$\left.\frac{d^2 c_1}{dr_1^2}\right|_{\dot{r}_1 = 0} = \frac{(1-\beta)(1-\alpha-\beta+\sigma)}{(\sigma-\alpha)^2} \frac{c_1}{r_1^2} > 0 \qquad (3.55)$$

We are now ready to analyze the phase diagrams for the two cases, corresponding to $\sigma < \alpha$ and $\sigma > \alpha$.

Case II: $\sigma < \alpha$

The phase diagram for this case is shown in Figure 3.3. The loci $\dot{r}_1 = 0$ and $\dot{c}_1 = 0$ divide the whole plane into four regions. The direction of the arrows in the various regions indicates the progression of the respective variables in those regions. Thus in region III $\dot{r}_1 < 0$ and $\dot{c}_1 > 0$. The intersection (r_1^∞, c_1^∞) of the loci is the steady state to which the system must approach. We show below that the steady state can only be approached along a path in the unshaded regions, as shown in Figure 3.3 by the heavy lines.

49

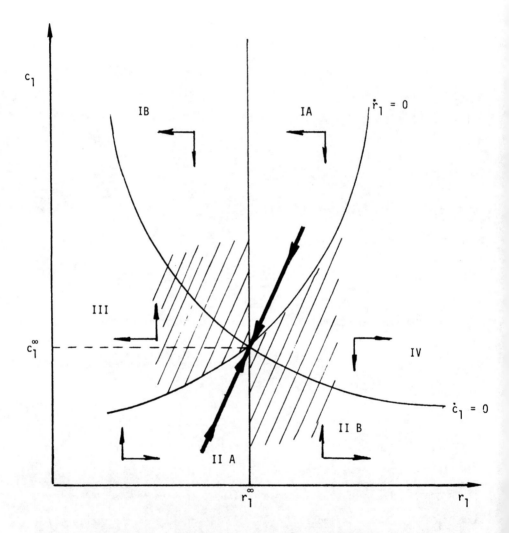

Figure 3.3: Phase Diagram in (r_1, c_1) Plane for $\sigma < \alpha$

Consider first the region III. In this region $\dot{r}_1 < 0$ and $\dot{c}_1 > 0$. From Figure 3.3 it is clear that a trajectory which once enters this region can neither get out of it nor can it converge to the steady state. In fact along a path in this region, in finite time we would have $r_1 = 0$, with c_1 increasing indefinitely-- which is clearly impossible. Hence the optimal path can not pass through the region III.

In region IV we have $\dot{r}_1 > 0$ and $\dot{c}_1 > 0$. As before it is easy to see that a trajectory, once in this region, always remains in this region and can never converge to the steady state. Hence this region must also be forbidden for the optimal trajectory.

Next in region IIB, i.e., the part of region II to the right of the vertical line through r_1^∞, we have $\dot{r}_1 > 0$ and $\dot{c}_1 > 0$. A trajectory once in this region can either remain in it or cross into region IV. In either case, however, it cannot approach the steady state. Similarly a trajectory in region IB, i.e., the part of region I to the left of the vertical line, can either remain in IB or can cross over into region II. Neither possibility leads to the steady state.

Thus we are left with the unshaded regions IA and IIA as the only regions through which a path can approach the steady state.

In region IIA, both c_1 and r_1 are increasing. Accordingly if the path remains in this region it must approach the steady state. Otherwise, the path leaves the region: it may either cross the line $r_1 = r_1^\infty$ or the boundary $\dot{r}_1 = 0$, eventually leading to non-optimality. We now show that for $c_1(0) < c_1^\infty$ there is exactly one value of

51

$r_1 = r_1(0)$ such that a path starting from $(r_1(0), c_1(0))$ will converge to the steady state (r_1^∞, c_1^∞).[7]

If we change the independent variable from t to c_1 then

$$\frac{c_1}{r_1} \frac{dr_1}{dc_1} = \frac{\dot{r}_1}{r_1} \bigg/ \frac{\dot{c}_1}{c_1} \qquad (3.56)$$

Now it can be easily shown that for a fixed c_1, $\frac{\dot{r}_1}{r_1}$ is an increasing function of r_1 while $\dot{c}_1/c_1$ is a decreasing function of r_1. Accordingly, $\frac{c_1}{r_1} \cdot \frac{dr_1}{dc_1}$ is, for a fixed c_1, an increasing function of r_1. Let $r_1'(c_1)$ and $r_1''(c_1)$ be the two trajectories with starting points $(r_1'(0), c_1(0))$ and $(r_1''(0), c_1(0))$ respectively. Then

$$\frac{d \ln[r_1'(c_1)/r_1''(c_1)]}{dc_1} = \frac{1}{c_1}\left[\frac{c_1}{r_1'} \frac{dr_1'}{dc_1} - \frac{c_1}{r_1''} \frac{dr_1''}{dc_1}\right] > 0$$

whenever $r_1'(c_1) > r_1''(c_1)$. Accordingly, if $r_1'(c_1(0)) = r_1'(0) > r_1''(0) = r_1''(c_1(0))$ then there can be no larger value of c_1 (within region IIA) for which $r_1'(c_1) \le r_1''(c_1)$, for in that case $\ln[r_1'(c_1)/r_1''(c_1)]$ would have to be decreasing at some smaller value of c_1, and this is impossible for the smallest such value. Hence $\ln[r_1'(c_1)/r_1''(c_1)]$ is increasing with c_1. In particular, as c_1 approaches c_1^∞ it is impossible that r_1' and r_1'' both approach the same limit r_1^∞. Thus, for any given $c_1(0)$, there can be at most one $r_1(0)$ from which the path approaches the steady state; by continuity there must be at least one. This point would then be the start of the only possible optimal path with initial controls $r_1(0)$ and $c_1(0)$.

---

[7]The following argument is essentially the same as used by Arrow and Kurz, in a somewhat different context, [4: pp. 69].

An exactly parallel argument applies in region IA. In that region c_1 and r_1 are decreasing. If a path remains in that region it must approach the steady state: this will occur along that solution of (3.56) which goes through (r_1^∞, c_1^∞).

By simple continuity considerations it is clear that for c_1 slightly greater than c_1^∞, there will be a r_1 such that the trajectory converges to (r_1^∞, c_1^∞). But then the solution to (3.56) can be continued for all value of c_1, for it is upward sloping and can cross neither $r_1 = r_1^\infty$, nor $\dot{r}_1 = 0$.

Thus we have established that for the normalized system to approach the steady state, the control r_1 and c_1 must be related to each other through a unique monotonical function $c_1 = c_1(r_1)$ with $\frac{dc_1}{dr_1} > 0$.

With $\dot{c}_1$, and $\dot{r}_1$, both having the same sign along the converging trajectory, it is obvious from (3.37a) that $\dot{k}_1$ would also have the same sign.

Lastly, the behaviour of x_1 along the optimal path can be found from a phase diagram of (3.37b) in the (r_1, x_1) plane. Such a diagram is shown in Figure 3.4, from which it is clear that along the converging path both $\dot{r}_1$ and $\dot{x}_1$ have the same sign.

Thus, along the converging trajectories all four variables k_1, x_1, r_1 and c_1 move in the same direction; they either monotonically decrease or increase to the steady state of the normalized system. We show below that the behavior of the first kind occurs when the economy starts with a relative capital abundance (i.e., $(k_1(0) > 1$, $x_1(0) = 1))$, while the behaviour of the second kind corresponds to a situation where capital is relatively scarce (i.e., $(k_1(0) < 1$, $x_1(0) = 1))$.

53

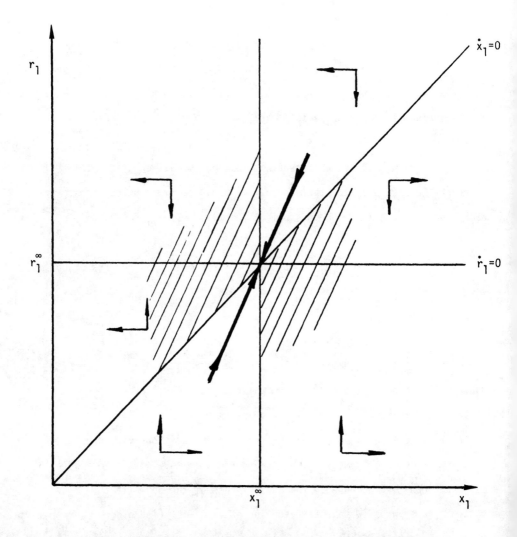

Figure 3.4: Phase Diagram in (r_1 , x_1) Plane

54

Assume to the contrary so that the system starting from $(k_1(0) > 1$, $x_1(0) = 1)$ approaches the steady state through monotonic increase. Then from eq. (3.37)

$$\frac{\dot{x}_1}{x_1} > 0 \rightarrow r_1(t) < x_1(t) \qquad (a)$$

$$\frac{\dot{c}_1}{c_1} > 0 \rightarrow k_1(t)^{\frac{1-\alpha}{\beta}} < r_1(t) \qquad (b) \qquad \left.\right\} \quad (3.57)$$

and

$$\frac{\dot{r}_1}{r_1} > 0 \rightarrow c_1(t) < k_1(t) \qquad (c)$$

Since in the steady state $c_1^\infty = k_1^\infty$ and $r_1^\infty = x_1^\infty$, it follows that for the system to approach the steady state, in some neighborhood of it, we must have

$$\frac{\dot{c}_1}{c_1} > \frac{\dot{k}_1}{k_1} \qquad (a)$$

$$\left.\right\} \quad (3.58)$$

$$\frac{\dot{r}_1}{r_1} > \frac{\dot{x}_1}{x_1} \qquad (b)$$

Combining (3.58a) with (3.37a), we have

$$\alpha \frac{\dot{k}_1}{k_1} > \sigma \frac{\dot{k}_1}{k_1} + (1-\beta) \frac{\dot{r}_1}{r_1}$$

or

$$\frac{\dot{k}_1}{k_1} > \frac{1-\beta}{\alpha-\sigma} \frac{\dot{r}_1}{r_1} \qquad (3.59)$$

Let $z_1 \equiv k_1^{\alpha-1} x_1^\beta$. Then

$$\frac{\dot{z}_1}{z_1} = -(1-\alpha) \frac{\dot{k}_1}{k_1} + \beta \frac{\dot{x}_1}{x_1}$$

Substituting from (3.58b) and (3.59)

$$\frac{\dot{z}_1}{z_1} < - \frac{(1-\alpha)\,(1-\beta)}{(\alpha-\sigma)} \frac{\dot{r}_1}{r_1} + \beta \frac{\dot{r}_1}{r_1}$$

or

$$\frac{\dot{z}_1}{z_1} < - \frac{(1-\alpha-\beta) + \sigma\beta}{(\alpha-\sigma)} \frac{\dot{r}_1}{r_1} < 0 \qquad\qquad (3.60)$$

Hence in some neighborhood of the steady state, z_1 decreases along the optimal trajectory. Now

$$z_1^\infty = (k_1^\infty)^{\alpha-1} (x_1^\infty)^\beta = 1 \qquad\qquad (\text{c.f. eq. (3.38)})$$

and therefore z_1 must have been greater than one before approaching the steady state. Furthermore, since

$$z_1(0) = k_1(0)^{\alpha-1} x_1(0)^\beta < 1 \; ,$$

by simple continuity argument z_1 must also be equal to one at some intermediate point along the trajectory. At that point

$$k_1^{\alpha-1} x_1^\beta = 1 \quad \text{or} \quad k_1^{\frac{1-\alpha}{\beta}} = x_1$$

But from (3.57), at any time t, we have

$$k_1^{\frac{1-\alpha}{\beta}} < r_1 < x_1$$

which is clearly impossible, and accordingly, our contention is proved.

Recall that in the steady state k_1^∞, x_1^∞, r_1^∞ and c_1^∞ are all less than one, equal to one or greater than one. Hence if the economy, starting from $(k_1(0)\,,\,1)$, monotonically increases to the steady state then in the steady state all four variables must be greater than one. Alternatively if the economy monotonically decreases to the steady state, then in the steady state all four variables must be less than one.

Thus, for an economy with relative capital abundance (i.e., $k_1(0) > 1$, $x_1(0) = 1$) initially, both k_1^∞ and x_1^∞ will be less than one. The optimal program will start with $c_1(0) > k_1(0)$ and $r_1(0) > x_1(0)$ and both k_1 and x_1 will decrease over time. The decrease in k_1 will be faster however, so that k_1 and x_1 will eventually be brought into conformity with each other. (See Figure 3.5 for typical trajectories.) In the long run, the economy behaves as if it had started with a balanced endowment corresponding to a resource stock lower than it actually had. Thus, as a result of the initial capital abundance, in the long run the economy behaves as if it had started with a capital stock and a resource stock both of which are smaller than the actual ones.

On the face of it, this is a rather surprising result; it implies, for example, that, in the long run, per capita consumption (and capital stock etc.) will be lower along a path which starts with a higher initial capital endowment and the same resource endowment. However, this seemingly counter-intuitive result has a rather simple explanation. Because of the complementarity of the capital and the exhaustible resource,

57

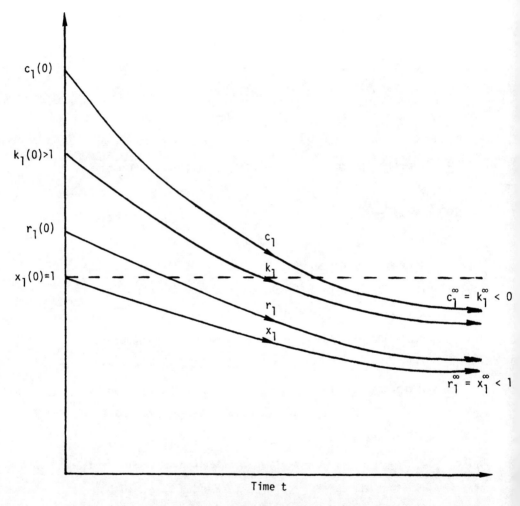

Figure 3.5: Typical Optimal Trajectories for 'Capital-Rich' Economies for $\sigma < \alpha$: Normalized Variables

it is better to use the resource at a time when the economy has a relatively high capital stock. This tendency, however, is offset by two
considerations: an increase in the resource usage rate results in a
lower marginal productivity for the resource, and any output in the
early periods is less valuable because of the fact that early generations
are relatively better off than the later ones.[8] In the present case
$\sigma < \alpha$, and the economy has relatively little egalitarian bias and does
not put much premium on the consumption of the poorer generations later
on. Thus, in the case of relatively high capital endowment, it dips into
the resource stock at a faster pace to give added consumption to the
early generations, at the cost of the later generations.

Just the opposite happens in the case of capital scarcity. The
optimal program starts with $c_1(0) < k_1(0)$ and $r_1(0) < x_1(0)$ and k_1
and x_1 increase over time. The increase in k_1 is faster, however,
so that once again k_1 and x_1 are brought into conformity eventually.
In the steady state, the system will be such that both k_1^{∞} and x_1^{∞} are
greater than one; accordingly, an economy, starting with a relative
capital scarcity, eventually behaves as if it had started with a higher
capital stock as well as a higher resource stock. (See Figure 3.6.)
The explanation for this behavior runs something like this: the relative capital scarcity indicates the need for a rapid capital formation,
which is done by curtailing the consumption initially; the complementarity
of the two inputs again means that it is better to use the resource later
on when through rapid capital formation, the economy has lessened its

---

[8]It should be emphasized that 'better' or 'worse' is in relation to
the 'balanced endowment' trajectories.

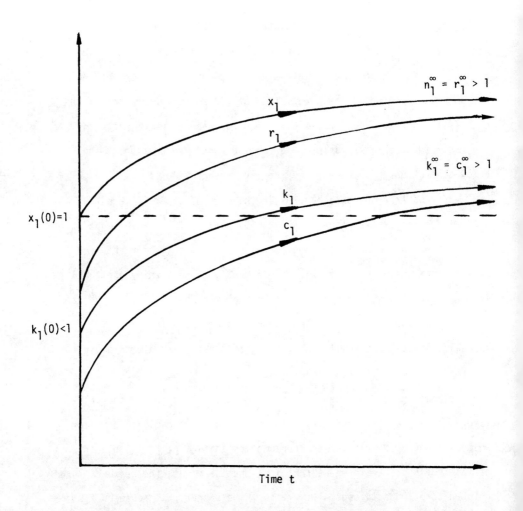

Figure 3.6: Typical Optimal Trajectories for 'Capital-Poor' Economies for $\sigma < \alpha$: Normalized Variables

60

capital scarcity, thus favoring the initial resource conservation. This initial sacrifice more than compensates for the initial capital deficiency so that eventually the economy behaves as if it had started at a higher base.

It ought to be emphasized here once more, that the long run superiority of a program starting from a lower capital stock and the same resource stock, is merely a result of the inter-temporal redistribution of consumption; overall, a program with higher capital stock will still be superior to the one with lower capital stock.[9]

As in the case of $\sigma = \alpha$, a parallel explanation can be provided for the above behavior, from the viewpoint of the relative resource availability.

Also, as before for $\sigma = \alpha$, it is possible to have optimal trajectories along which per capita consumption and capital increase for a while and then decrease to the steady state subsequently. The consumption will increase whenever $\frac{\dot{c}_1}{c_1} > |\gamma_1|$ while the capital will increase whenever $\frac{\dot{k}_1}{k_1} > |\gamma_1|$. Since for this case $\frac{\dot{c}_1}{c_1} > \frac{\dot{k}_1}{k_1}$, it is possible that the consumption will increase for some time even while capital is decreasing.

Figures 3.7(a)-(d) show the typical optimal behavior for k, x, c and r for 'capital-rich', 'capital-poor' and 'balanced endowments' economies.

Case III: $\sigma > \alpha$

From (3.53) and (3.55) it is easy to show that, for $\sigma > \alpha$, at the intersection of the two loci $\dot{r}_1 = 0$ and $\dot{c}_1 = 0$ we have

---

[9]Otherwise the shadow price of capital would have to be negative.

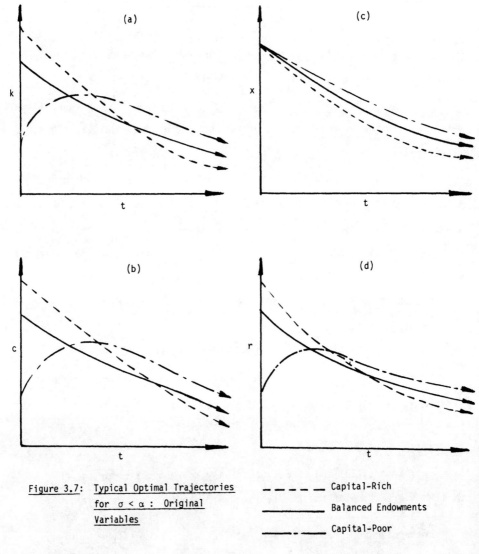

Figure 3.7: Typical Optimal Trajectories
for σ < α : Original
Variables

Capital-Rich

Balanced Endowments

Capital-Poor

62

$$\frac{dc_1}{dr_1}\bigg|_{\dot{c}_1 = 0} > \frac{dc_1}{dr_1}\bigg|_{\dot{r}_1 = 0} \qquad\qquad (3.61)$$

i.e., for (3.61) to hold we must have

$$-\frac{1-\alpha-\beta}{\sigma(1-\alpha)} > -\frac{1-\beta}{\sigma-\alpha}$$

or $\qquad\qquad (\sigma-\alpha)(1-\alpha-\beta) < \alpha(1-\beta)(1-\alpha)$

or $\qquad\qquad \sigma(1-\alpha-\beta) - \alpha(1-\alpha-\beta) < \sigma(1-\alpha-\beta) + \sigma\alpha\beta$

or $\qquad\qquad 0 < \sigma\alpha\beta + \alpha(1-\alpha-\beta)$

which is true.

The phase diagram for this case is shown in Figure 3.8. The loci $\dot{r}_1 = 0$ and $\dot{c}_1 = 0$ divide the whole plane into four regions. The direction of the arrows in the various regions indicates the progression of the respective variables in those regions. Thus in region I, $\dot{r}_1 < 0$ and $\dot{c}_1 > 0$. The intersection (c_1^∞, r_1^∞) of the loci is the steady state to which the system must converge.

Using an argument exactly parallel to the one used for $\sigma < \alpha$ we can show that the steady state can only be approached along a path in the unshaded region, as shown in Figure 3.8 by heavy lines; and also that for the normalized system to approach the steady state, the controls r_1 and c_1 must be such that they are related to each other through a unique monotonically decreasing function $c_1 = c_1(r_1)$ with $\frac{dc_1}{dr_1} < 0$.

The phase diagram of (3.37b) in the (r_1, x_1) plane shown in Figure 3.4, is still applicable and hence along the converging trajectory both r_1 and x_1 still move in the same direction.

Thus, along the optimal trajectory, $\dot{x}_1$ and $\dot{r}_1$ have the same sign while the sign of $\dot{c}_1$ is opposite to theirs. With $\dot{c}_1$ and $\dot{r}_1$

63

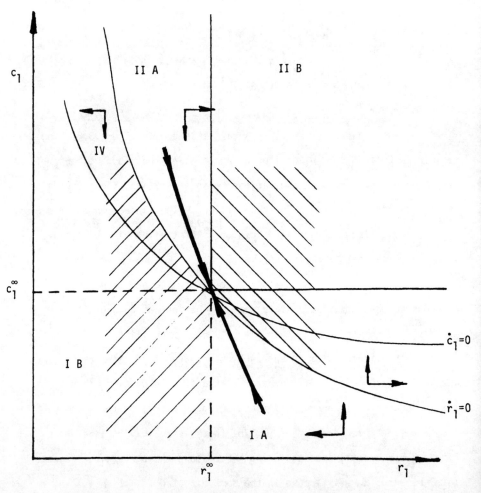

Figure 3.8: Phase Diagram in (r_1, c_1) Plane for $\sigma > \alpha$

64

having opposite signs, we can no longer use (3.37a) to establish the sign of $\dot{k}_1$. However, as we show below, $\dot{k}_1$ would have the same sign as $\dot{c}_1$.

Consider the case when $\dot{r}_1 > 0$ and $\dot{c}_1 < 0$. Then for $\dot{r}_1 > 0$ we must have $\frac{c_1(t)}{k_1(t)} < 1$. Since in the steady state $\frac{c_1^\infty}{k_1^\infty} = 1$, it follows that in some neighborhood of the steady state we must have

$$\dot{v}_1 = \frac{\dot{c}_1}{c_1} - \frac{\dot{k}_1}{k_1} > 0 \tag{3.62}$$

where

$$v_1 = \frac{c_1}{k_1}$$

Suppose (3.62) does not hold all along the optimal trajectory so that for some time interval, $\dot{v}_1 < 0$. Thus v_1 first decreases, reaches a minimum and increases subsequently. Accordingly, v_1 will take some value $\bar{v}_1$ at two different times t_1 and $t_2 (> t_1)$. Using the superscripts to denote time we have

$$\frac{\dot{c}_1^1}{c_1^1} < \frac{\dot{k}_1^1}{k_1^1} \quad \text{and} \quad \frac{\dot{c}_1^2}{c_1^2} > \frac{\dot{k}_1^2}{k_1^2}$$

or

$$\frac{\dot{c}_1^2}{c_1^2} - \frac{\dot{c}_1^1}{c_1^1} > \frac{\dot{k}_1^2}{k_1^2} - \frac{\dot{k}_1^1}{k_1^1} \qquad . \tag{3.63}$$

65

From (3.37d)

$$\frac{\dot{r}_1^1}{r_1^1} = \frac{\dot{r}_1^2}{r_1^2}$$

and then from (3.37a)

$$\frac{\dot{k}_1^2}{k_1^2} - \frac{\dot{k}_1^1}{k_1^1} = \frac{\sigma}{\alpha}\left[\frac{\dot{c}_1^2}{c_1^2} - \frac{\dot{c}_1^1}{c_1^1}\right] \quad .$$

Combining with (3.63)

$$\frac{\dot{c}_1^2}{c_1^2} - \frac{\dot{c}_1^1}{c_1^1} > \frac{\sigma}{\alpha}\left[\frac{\dot{c}_1^2}{c_1^2} - \frac{\dot{c}_1^1}{c_1^1}\right] \quad . \tag{3.64}$$

Since $\sigma > \alpha$, it follows from (3.64) that

$$\frac{\dot{c}_1^2}{c_1^2} - \frac{\dot{c}_1^1}{c_1^1} < 0 \quad . \tag{3.65}$$

However from (3.37c)

$$\frac{\dot{c}_1^2}{c_1^2} - \frac{\dot{c}_1^1}{c_1^1} = \frac{\sigma\gamma_k + (\mu+\delta)}{\sigma} \cdot (\bar{v}_1)^{1-\alpha}\left[\frac{(r_1^2)^\beta}{(c_1^2)^{1-\alpha}} - \frac{(r_1^1)^\beta}{(c_1^1)^{1-\alpha}}\right] > 0$$

as

$$r_1^2 > r_1^1$$

and

$$c_1^2 < c_1^1$$

66

Accordingly, we have a contradiction and hence (3.62) is valid all along the trajectory.

Similarly we can prove that when $\dot{c}_1 > 0$ then $\dfrac{\dot{k}_1}{k_1} > \dfrac{\dot{c}_1}{c_1} > 0$.

Thus, along the converging trajectory we have either $\dot{c}_1 > 0$, $\dot{k}_1 > 0$, $\dot{r}_1 < 0$ and $\dot{x}_1 < 0$; or $\dot{c}_1 < 0$, $\dot{k}_1 < 0$, $\dot{r}_1 > 0$ and $\dot{x}_1 > 0$. It is easy to see that the first case occurs when the economy starts with a relative capital scarcity $(k_1(0) < 1$, $x_1(0) = 1)$ and the second when capital is relatively abundant $(k_1(0) > 1$, $x_1(0) = 1)$.

Assume to the contrary, for example, so that in case of capital scarcity we have $\dot{c}_1 < 0$, $\dot{k}_1 < 0$, $\dot{r}_1 > 0$ and $\dot{x}_1 > 0$. Then in steady state we have

$$k_1^{\infty} < k_1(0) < 1$$

and

$$x_1^{\infty} > x_1(0) = 1$$

However, we observed earlier that in steady state we must have either both greater than one or less than one. Thus, reductio ad absurdum, our original contention is correct.

Figures 3.9 and 3.10 show the typical trajectories for $\sigma > \alpha$, in terms of the normalized variable. Figures 3.11(a)-(d) show the same in terms of the original variable.

If capital is abundant, the optimal program starts with $c_1(0) < k_1(0)$ and $r_1(0) < x_1(0)$.[10] In the long run the economy behaves

---

[10] From Figures 3.9 and 3.10 it may seem that because after sometime the trajecectories of k_1 and x_1 cross-over, the economy has reversed its relative endowment. However, this is not true as for $k_1 \neq 1$, $x_1 = k_1$ is not the balanced endowment (cf. eq. (3.38)).

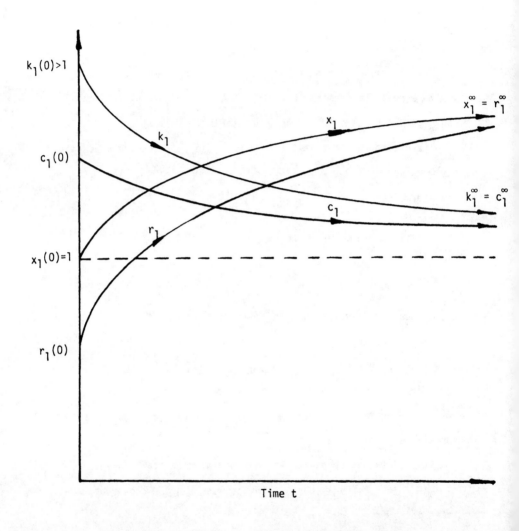

Figure 3.9: Typical Optimal Trajectories for 'Capital-Rich' Economies for $\sigma > \alpha$: Normalized Variables

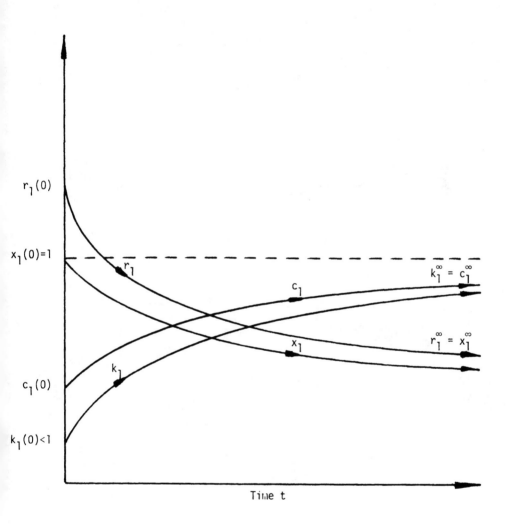

Figure 3.10: Typical Optimal Trajectories for "Capital-Poor' Economies
for $(\sigma > \alpha)$: Normalized Variables

69

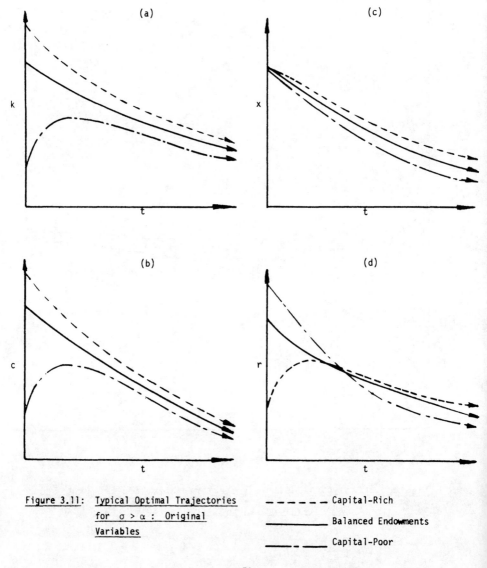

Figure 3.11: Typical Optimal Trajectories for $\sigma > \alpha$: Original Variables

— — — — — Capital-Rich

——————— Balanced Endowments

— · — · — Capital-Poor

70

as if it had started with a lower than actual capital endowment and with a higher than actual resource endowment. This is in contrast to the case for $\sigma < \alpha$ where in the long run a capital abundant economy behaved as if it had started with lower capital as well as with lower resource stock. The difference is explained by the fact that due to $\sigma > \alpha$, the higher egalitarian bias dominates the effects of complementarity of the resource with the capital. The economy cuts down the resource usage initially, to preserve it for the poorer generations later on.

A capital scarce economy on the other hand starts with $c_1(0) > k_1(0)$ and $r_1(0) > x_1(0)$. In the long run the economy behaves as if it has started with a higher capital stock and a lower resource stock. This is again in contrast to the case for $\sigma < \alpha$ where in the long run a capital scarce economy behaved as if it started with higher capital as well as a higher resource stock. As before, the difference is due to the fact that egalitarian considerations dominate the complementarity considerations. Thus rather than to preserve the resource initially to use it later when capital is no longer deficient, the economy uses it at a faster pace initially, to give added consumption to the relatively poor early generations.

Summary of the Results for the Three Cases

Since in the long run even an economy with unbalanced initial endowment behaves as if it had started with some balanced endowment, it is possible to describe the long run behavior in terms of equivalent balanced endowments. This is done in Figure 3.12. The curve OM is the locus representing the balanced endowment (c.f. eq. (3.31)). Any

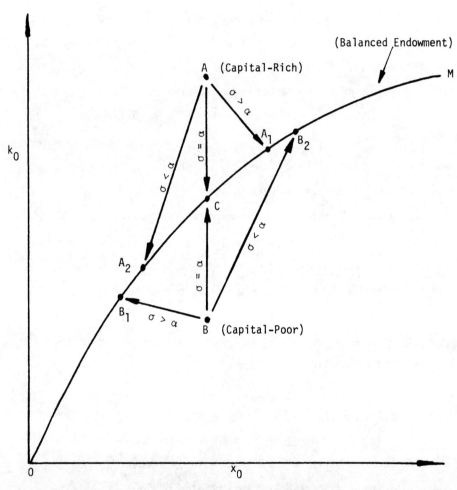

Figure 3.12: Dependence of the Long Run Behavior on σ

72

endowment corresponding to a point above this locus represents a relatively capital-rich economy while an endowment below the locus corresponds to a capital-poor economy. Points A , B and C represent three economies starting with the same resource stock but different capital stocks. A is relatively capital-rich; B is relatively capital-poor and C has a balanced endowment. If $\sigma = \alpha$ then the economies starting at A and B behave as if they had started at C . Points A_1 , A_2 , B_1 and B_2 describe the behavior of the capital-rich and capital-poor economies for $\sigma \neq \alpha$.[11]

3.1.5 Numerical Examples

To give some perspective to the results for the 'unbalanced endowments', we return to the numerical example in Section 3.1.3. The values for all the basic parameters except σ are assumed to be the same as before. However, in order to cover the three cases corresponding

---

[11]The counter-intuitive behavior, for $\sigma < \alpha$, where in the long run a capital-poor economy is better off than a capital-rich economy, raises interesting questions about the choice of σ , the elasticity of marginal utility of consumption. Insofar as the appropriate test for the suitability of an ethical judgment is the sensibleness of its implications, the previous analysis seems to suggest choosing $\sigma > \alpha$. Thus for example, suppose we impose an additional value judgment that no future generation should suffer merely because of an increase in the initial capital stock of their predecessors, i.e., if c'(t) and c"(t) were the consumption trajectories for two economies starting with (k'(0), x(0)) and (k"(0) , x(0)) respectively, then

$$c'(t) \geq c''(t) \quad \text{for all} \quad t$$

provided $$k'(0) > k''(0).$$

This assumption then precludes the possibility of choosing $\sigma < \alpha$. This is in contrast to the traditional neo-classical growth theory models where no such restriction on the value of σ is necessary. Interestingly, Chakravarty [8] in analyzing some finite-horizon models,numerically, finds it necessary to use values of σ as high as 4 , to get reasonable savings rates. Since $\alpha < 1$, values of that order for σ would, of course, be more than enough to eliminate the somewhat uncomfortable behaviour of the optimal trajectories.

to $\sigma < \alpha$, $\sigma = \alpha$, and $\sigma > \alpha$, we shall use three different values
(0.1, 0.25 and 1.0) for σ . To the extent that the values of the
various parameters characterizing the 'balanced endowment' paths depend
upon σ , they will differ for the three cases. Their values for
$x_* = 1,000$ are shown below:

Parameter	$\sigma = 0.1$	$\sigma = 0.25$	$\sigma = 1.0$
k_*	5.408	5.427	5.510
c_*	1.359	1.357	1.344
r_*	11.915	11.579	10.000
$\gamma_k = \gamma_c$	-0.0021	-0.0021	-0.0020
$\gamma_x = \gamma_r$	-0.0319	-0.0316	-0.0300

Notice that the 'balanced endowments' parameters are relatively
insensitive to changes in the value of σ .

For illustrative purposes, the endowments of the 'capital-poor'
economy are assumed to be $(k_0 = 2.5$, $x_0 = 1,000)$ and those for the
'capital-rich' economy to $(k_0 = 10$, $x_0 = 1,000)$. The progression of
the optimal trajectories for these economies, for the three values of σ ,
are shown in Tables 1 through 3. Summarized below are some of the more
interesting characteristics of these trajectories.

i) The non-monotonic behavior, predicted in the analysis
earlier, is very much in evidence. For $\sigma = 0.25$ $(=\alpha)$, for example,
the capital stock increases from 2.5 to about 5.2, before it starts declining towards the steady state value of zero.

ii) Shown below are the equivalent initial endowments, indicated
by the long run behavior of the economies, for various cases.

Table 1:   Examples of Optimal Trajectories for $\sigma = 0.25$ $(=\alpha)$

(i) Capital-Poor Economy: $k_0 = 2.5$, $x_0 = 1{,}000$

t	k_1	x_1	c_1/k_1	r_1/x_1	k	x	c	r
0	0.4606	1.0000	1.0000	1.0000	2.5000	1000.00	0.6250	11.5789
2	0.6537	1.0000	1.0000	1.0000	3.5325	938.79	0.8831	10.8702
4	0.7312	1.0000	1.0000	1.0000	4.2040	881.33	1.0510	10.2049
6	0.8629	1.0000	1.0000	1.0000	4.6243	827.39	1.1560	9.5803
8	0.9145	1.0000	1.0000	1.0000	4.8802	776.75	1.2200	8.9939
10	0.9469	1.0000	1.0000	1.0000	5.0314	729.21	1.2578	8.4435
12	0.9670	1.0000	1.0000	1.0000	5.1169	684.58	1.2792	7.9267
14	0.9795	1.0000	1.0000	1.0000	5.1614	642.68	1.2903	7.4415
16	0.9873	1.0000	1.0000	1.0000	5.1305	603.34	1.2951	6.9861
18	0.9921	1.0000	1.0000	1.0000	5.1839	566.41	1.2959	6.5585
20	0.9951	1.0000	1.0000	1.0000	5.1776	531.75	1.2944	6.1571
→∞	1.0000	1.0000	1.0000	1.0000	→0	→0	→0	→0

(ii) Capital-Rich Economy: $k_0 = 10.0$, $x_0 = 1{,}0000$

t	k_1	x_1	c_1/k_1	r_1/x_1	k	x	c	r
0	1.3427	1.0000	1.0000	1.0000	10.0000	1000.00	2.5000	11.5789
2	1.5066	1.0000	1.0000	1.0000	8.1415	938.79	2.0353	10.8702
4	1.3074	1.0000	1.0000	1.0000	7.0357	881.33	1.7589	10.2049
6	1.1878	1.0000	1.0000	1.0000	6.3652	827.39	1.5913	9.5803
8	1.1153	1.0000	1.0000	1.0000	5.9514	776.75	1.4878	8.9939
10	1.0710	1.0000	1.0000	1.0000	5.6909	729.21	1.4227	8.4435
12	1.0438	1.0000	1.0000	1.0000	5.5230	684.58	1.3807	7.9267
14	1.0270	1.0000	1.0000	1.0000	5.4116	642.68	1.3529	7.4415
16	1.0167	1.0000	1.0000	1.0000	5.3346	603.34	1.3336	6.9861
18	1.0103	1.0000	1.0000	1.0000	5.2789	566.41	1.3197	6.5585
20	1.0063	1.0000	1.0000	1.0000	5.2351	531.75	1.3090	5.1571
→∞	1.0000	1.0000	1.0000	1.0000	→0	→0	→0	→0

Table 2: Examples of Optimal Trajectories for $\sigma = 0.10$ $(<\alpha)$

(i) Capital-Poor Economy: $k_0 = 2.5$, $x_0 = 1{,}000$

t	k_1	x_1	c_1/k_1	r_1/x_1	k	x	c	r
0	0.4622	1.0000	0.5934	0.9350	2.5000	1000.00	0.3759	11.1404
2	0.7207	1.0011	0.8197	0.9690	3.3815	939.19	0.7995	10.8440
4	0.8636	1.0016	0.9179	0.9847	4.6315	881.59	1.0683	10.3441
6	0.9352	1.0019	0.9623	0.9920	4.9940	827.29	1.2075	9.7786
8	0.9696	1.0020	0.9825	0.9953	5.1557	776.25	1.2729	9.2061
10	0.9858	1.0021	0.9919	0.9968	5.2197	728.32	1.3009	8.6509
12	0.9934	1.0022	0.9962	0.9975	5.2375	683.33	1.3111	8.1221
14	0.9969	1.0022	0.9982	0.9978	5.2338	641.11	1.3128	7.6225
16	0.9986	1.0023	0.9991	0.9979	5.2203	601.49	1.3106	7.1524
18	0.9994	1.0023	0.9995	0.9980	5.2022	564.32	1.3065	6.7107
20	0.9998	1.0024	0.9996	0.9980	5.1822	529.45	1.3016	6.2960
$\to \infty$	1.00004	1.00059	1.0000	1.0000	$\to 0$	$\to 0$	$\to 0$	$\to 0$

(ii) Capital-Rich Economy: $k_c = 10.0$, $x_0 = 1{,}000$

t	k_1	x_1	c_1/k_1	r_1/x_1	k	x	c	r
0	1.3439	1.0000	1.3535	1.0670	10.0000	1000.00	3.4011	12.7132
2	1.3559	0.9933	1.1745	1.0325	7.3027	937.09	2.1552	11.5285
4	1.1573	0.9932	1.0332	1.0162	6.2065	878.65	1.3893	10.6387
6	1.0713	0.9930	1.0391	1.0085	5.7210	824.03	1.4938	9.9032
8	1.0327	0.9978	1.0182	1.0050	5.4915	773.00	1.4051	9.2569
10	1.0151	0.9977	1.0085	1.0034	5.3748	725.13	1.3620	8.6697
12	1.0069	0.9976	1.0039	1.0027	5.3091	680.25	1.3393	8.1271
14	1.0032	0.9976	1.0025	1.0024	5.2667	638.24	1.3258	7.6217
16	1.0014	0.9975	1.0009	1.0022	5.2352	598.64	1.3166	7.1492
18	1.0006	0.9975	1.0005	1.0022	5.2086	561.60	1.3094	6.7065
20	1.0002	0.9974	1.0004	1.0022	5.1842	526.84	1.3032	6.2914
$\to \infty$	0.99998	0.99967	1.0000	1.0000	$\to 0$	$\to 0$	$\to 0$	$\to 0$

76

Table 3: Examples of Optimal Trajectories for $\sigma = 1.0$ $(>\alpha)$

(i) Capital-Poor Economy: $k_0 = 2.5$, $x_0 = 1,000$

t	k_1	x_1	c_1/k_1	r_1/x_1	k	x	c	r
0	0.4537	1.0000	1.4961	1.1950	2.5000	1000.00	0.9126	11.9500
2	0.5654	0.9967	1.3335	1.1375	3.1027	933.66	1.0095	10.6675
4	0.6549	0.9943	1.2361	1.0995	3.5800	881.13	1.0797	9.6975
6	0.7264	0.9926	1.1723	1.0731	3.9549	829.13	1.1313	8.8977
8	0.7833	0.9913	1.1283	1.0540	4.2476	779.86	1.1694	8.2200
10	0.8285	0.9904	1.0967	1.0399	4.4747	733.75	1.1974	7.6306
12	0.8644	0.9897	1.0735	1.0293	4.6499	690.55	1.2179	7.1083
14	0.8929	0.9892	1.0559	1.0213	4.7841	650.00	1.2326	6.6391
16	0.9156	0.9889	1.0425	1.0153	4.8361	611.92	1.2428	6.2131
18	0.9337	0.9836	1.0319	1.0107	4.9629	576.14	1.2496	5.8234
20	0.9433	0.9834	1.0235	1.0073	5.0200	542.49	1.2537	5.4643
→ ∞	0.9936	0.9796	1.0000	1.0000	0	0	0	0

(ii) Capital-Rich Economy: $k_0 = 10.0$, $x_0 = 1,000$

t	k_1	x_1	c_1/k_1	r_1/x_1	k	x	c	r
0	1.3149	1.0000	0.7515	0.8590	10.0000	1000.00	1.8337	8.5900
2	1.6422	1.0025	0.7876	0.8825	9.0113	944.20	1.7319	8.3328
4	1.5061	1.0047	0.8205	0.9030	8.2325	891.12	1.6482	8.0475
6	1.3991	1.0065	0.8499	0.9207	7.6167	840.70	1.5795	7.7410
8	1.3147	1.0079	0.8757	0.9357	7.1291	792.88	1.5233	7.4197
10	1.2433	1.0091	0.8979	0.9433	6.7413	747.57	1.4771	7.0899
12	1.1959	1.0100	0.9163	0.9588	6.4332	704.69	1.4392	6.7568
14	1.1546	1.0108	0.9327	0.9674	6.1861	664.14	1.4079	6.4250
16	1.1220	1.0113	0.9460	0.9744	5.9373	625.83	1.3820	6.0981
18	1.0962	1.0118	0.9570	0.9800	5.8264	589.65	1.3605	5.7738
20	1.0753	1.0122	0.9660	0.9845	5.6950	555.51	1.3424	5.4692
→ ∞	1.0011	1.0172	1.0000	1.0000	0	0	0	0

77

	Actual Endowment	Equivalent Endowment		
		$\sigma > \alpha$	$\sigma = \alpha$	$\sigma > \alpha$
'capital-poor'	(2.500, 1,000.0)	(5.409, 1,000.6)	(5.426, 1,000)	(5.502, 979.
'capital-rich'	(10.000, 1,000.0)	(5.408, 997.7)	(5.426, 1,000)	(5.516, 1,017.

Thus the counter-intuitive 'rich-poor' reversal for $\sigma < \alpha$ is more of an analytical anomaly; in practical terms, it is rather unimportant.[12]

Notice that even for $\sigma \neq \alpha$, the long run equivalent resource endowment is very close to the actual resource endowment. Any original imbalance in endowments is corrected essentially through appropriate adjustments to the capital.

iii) The normalized variables are within a few percent of their steady state values by the 20th period,[13] indicating a tendency to rapidly correct any original imbalance.[14] Thus any imbalance in the endowments would be a short lived phenomenon; after a few periods, the balanced endowment solution would represent a very close approximation to the actual solution.

The combined effect of (ii) and (iii) is to relegate the initial capital endowment to a rather passive role, important only for

---

[12]Increasing the original imbalance makes the reversal somewhat more pronounced, though still not very significant, in practical terms.

[13]For the values of the parameters assumed in this example, the period would be roughly a year long.

[14]Even a relatively drastic imbalance gets corrected rapidly. For example, starting from $(k_1(0) = .01$, $x_1(0) = 1)$, the solution would again be within a few percent of the balanced endowment solution by the 25th period.

78

determining the solution for a few periods in the beginning. If capital
is relatively scarce then consumption is curtailed for rapid capital
accumulation; if capital is relatively abundant then the excess capital
is quickly dissipated through extra consumption. The initial resource
stock determines the subsequent behavior for approach to the null steady
state. Thus, while in the steady state neither the initial capital stock
nor the initial resource stock is of any importance; the former is
essentially unimportant even for governing the behavior during approach
to the steady state.

3.2 Cobb-Douglas Technology with Technical Progress

In the analysis so far we assumed the absence of any technical
progress and not unexpectedly found that the economy constrained by the
finite stock of the exhaustible resource, settled down on a declining
path for the eventual rendezvous with the doom's day. As we show below,
this need not be so; given adequate technical progress, the economy can
maintain a constant standard of living or can even improve it over time.

3.2.1 The Modified Model

Let τ be the expontential rate of the Hicks neutral technical
progress[15] so that the production function, in per capita terms, is

$$y(t) = e^{\tau t} \, k(t)^{\alpha} \cdot r(t)^{\beta} \qquad (3.66)$$

---

[15]Alternatively this can be considered as a resource augmenting
technical change at the exponential rate of τ/β .

Proceeding exactly as we did for the static technology case, it can be shown that instead of (3.13), the optimal trajectories would now need to satisfy

$$\frac{\dot{k}}{k} = e^{\tau t}\, k^{\alpha-1}\, r^{\beta} - (\mu+n) - \frac{c}{k} \qquad\qquad (a)$$

$$\frac{\dot{x}}{x} = -\left(\frac{r}{x} + n\right) \qquad\qquad\qquad\qquad (b)$$

$$\frac{\dot{c}}{c} = \frac{1}{\sigma}\left[\alpha\, e^{\tau t}\, k^{\alpha-1}\, r^{\beta} - (\mu+\delta)\right] \qquad (c)$$

$$\frac{\dot{r}}{r} = \frac{1}{1-\beta}\left\{\alpha\frac{\dot{k}}{k} - \sigma\frac{\dot{c}}{c} - (\delta - \tau)\right\} \qquad (d)$$

$$\left.\begin{array}{c} \\ \\ \\ \\ \\ \\ \end{array}\right\}(3.67)$$

3.2.2 Optimal Trajectories from Balanced Endowments

The analysis of (3.67) differs from that of (3.13) only in one respect; the rate constants $\gamma_k \ldots \gamma_r$ for (3.67) are different from those for (3.13). It is easy to show that now

$$\gamma_k^{\tau} = \gamma_c^{\tau} = \frac{-\delta\beta + \tau}{1 - \alpha - \beta + \sigma\beta}$$

$$= \gamma_k\left(1 - \frac{\tau}{\delta\beta}\right) = \gamma_c\left(1 - \frac{\tau}{\delta\beta}\right) \qquad (3.68)$$

and

$$\gamma_x^{\tau} = \gamma_r^{\tau} = \frac{-\delta(1-\alpha) + \tau(1-\sigma)}{(1 - \alpha - \beta + \sigma\beta)}$$

$$= \gamma_x\left(1 - \frac{\tau(1-\sigma)}{\delta(1-\alpha)}\right) = \gamma_r\left(1 - \frac{\tau(1-\sigma)}{\delta(1-\alpha)}\right) \qquad (3.69)$$

where the superscript τ distinguishes the present parameters from those obtained previously for the static technology case. Thus the four rate constants $\gamma_c^{\tau} \ldots \gamma_c^{\tau}$, in addition to being dependent upon α, β, σ and δ, also depend upon τ, the rate of technical progress. Notice that if $\tau > \tau^* = \delta\beta$, then γ_k^{τ} and γ_c^{τ} will be positive and

80

accordingly the capital stock and the consumption will increase over time. This is in contrast to the situation in the no-technical progress case where the capital and the consumption always decreased in the long run. τ^* is thus the minimum critical rate of technical progress necessary to ensure a non-zero steady state.

Notice also that γ_x^τ and γ_r^τ still remain negative and hence once again, no conflict need arise with the finiteness of the resource endowment.[16]

The relations (3.28)-(3.31) between the constants c_*, k_*, r_* and x_*, along the balanced endowment paths will be still valid, provided we replace the static technology 'gammas' from (3.22) and (3.24) with those from (3.68) and (3.69). Thus now the balanced endowments will be given by

$$x_*^\tau = \frac{1}{[-(\gamma_x^\tau + n)]} \left[\frac{\sigma\gamma_k^\tau + (\mu + \delta)}{\alpha} \right]^{\frac{1}{\beta}} (k_*^\tau)^{\frac{1-\alpha}{\beta}} \quad {}^{17} \qquad (3.70)$$

and for a balanced endowment we would have

$$c_*^\tau = \left[\frac{(\sigma-\alpha)\gamma_k^\tau + (\mu+\delta)}{\alpha} - (\mu + n) \right] k_*^\tau \qquad (3.71)$$

and
$$r_*^\tau = - (\gamma_x^\tau + n)x_*^\tau \qquad (3.72)$$

---

[16]It is easily shown, however, that for the convergence of the welfare functional (2.10), δ must be such that

$$\delta(1-\alpha) - \tau(1-\sigma) > n(1-\alpha-\beta+\sigma\beta) \quad \text{(c.f. footnote 2).}$$

[17]Notice that even a Hicks neutral technical progress will, in general,

81

The optimal savings rate along a balanced endowment solution will be given by

$$s = \frac{\alpha(\gamma_k^\tau + \mu+n)}{\sigma\gamma_k^\tau + \mu + \delta} \qquad (3.73)$$

For comparison the optimal steady state savings ratio $\bar{s}$, in the traditional growth models (i.e., with $\beta = 0$) is given by [18]

$$\bar{s} = \frac{\alpha(\mu + n)}{\mu + \delta} + \frac{\alpha}{1-\alpha}\frac{\tau}{\mu - \delta} \qquad (3.74)$$

From (3.73) and (3.74)

$$s - \bar{s} = \frac{\alpha}{\mu + \delta}\frac{\gamma_k^\tau[(\mu + \delta) - (\mu + n)\sigma]}{\sigma\gamma_k^\tau + \mu + \delta} - \frac{\tau}{1-\alpha} \qquad (3.75)$$

Depending upon the values of the basic parameters of the economy, the R.H.S. of (3.75) can be positive, negative or zero. For example, if $\tau = 0$ then $s \gtrless \bar{s}$ accordingly as

$$\sigma \gtrless \frac{\mu + \delta}{\mu + n}$$

Thus, contrary to Anderson's [3] conclusion, the optimal savings rate in resource constrained formulation is not necessarily lower than that for the non-resource constrained problem. Notice, however,

---

shift the locus of the balanced endowments; the direction of the shift will depend upon the values of the basic parameters of the economy.

[18]See, for example, Shell [33]. Notice that because of a minor difference between our criterion functional and that used by Shell, the expression given here is slightly different from his.

82

that if $\sigma = 0$, as is implicit in the linear utility function used by Anderson, then (3.75) reduces to

$$s - \bar{s} = \frac{\alpha}{\mu + \delta} \left[\gamma_k^\tau - \frac{\tau}{1-\alpha} \right] < 0$$

which explains his conclusion about the lower savings rate.

3.2.3 Optimal Trajectories from Arbitrary Endowments

It is easy to show that the normalized system for (3.67) would be exactly the same as for the static technology case and accordingly all the results pertaining to the normalized variables would still be applicable.

The behavior of the optimal trajectories, in terms of the actual variables, will, of course, depend upon τ . If $\tau < \tau^*$ then all the 'gammas' will still be negative and the optimal trajectories will essentially be the same as before; the only difference being that now capital and consumption will decline at a slower pace while the resource would be exhausted at a faster pace.

For $\tau > \tau^*$ however, the optimal capital and consumption trajectories will differ qualitatively from those for the static technology case. The secular downward trend experienced earlier for these trajectories will now be changed into an upward trend, and accordingly, in the long run, the economy will enjoy an ever increasing standard of living.

The possibility of non-monotonic behavior of capital and consumption would still exist. However, now this would happen

83

for 'capital-rich' economies rather than for the 'capital-poor' economies. For example, it can be shown that along the optimal trajectories, for an economy starting with $(k_1(0)\,,\,1)$ where

$$k_1(0) > \left[\frac{\sigma Y_k^\tau + (\mu + \delta)}{(\mu + \delta)} \right]^{\frac{1}{1-\alpha}} \tag{3.76}$$

capital and consumption will decline initially, only to increase later on. See Figures 3.13-3.15, for some typical optimal trajectories, in terms of the actual variables.

A Brief Summary

In summary then, the introduction of exponential technical progress leaves the earlier analysis practically unchanged. The change in the nature of the long run solution can be very basic however; for any progress below the minimum critical rate of progress there is no escape from the doom's day, while if the rate of progress exceeds the critical rate then even with a finite endowment of an essential resource, the economy would be able to sustain an ever improving standard of living.[19]

---

[19]From this perspective the current debate about the future availability of the exhaustible resources would seem to be largely misdirected. In the long run, neither a large current stock of these resources nor a curtailment of the current consumption can avoid the doom's day; only technical progress can do so. The crucial questions, for the debate, should then be the magnitude and nature of technical progress as well as the mechanism through which technical change is brought about.

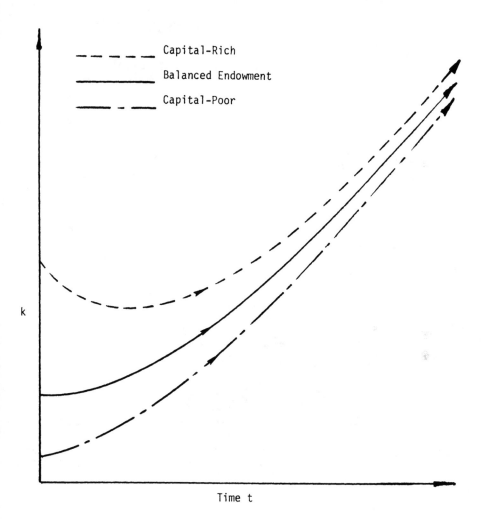

Capital-Rich

Balanced Endowment

Capital-Poor

k

Time t

<u>Figure 3.13</u>:   <u>Typical Optimal Trajectories for Capital Stock</u>
<u>for $\sigma = \alpha$ and $\tau > \tau^*$</u>

85

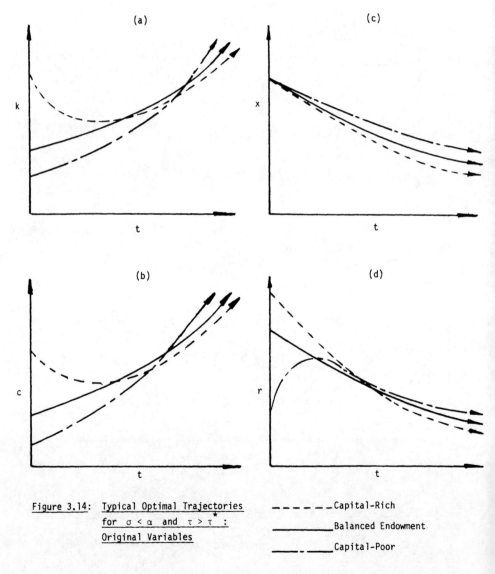

Figure 3.14: Typical Optimal Trajectories
for $\sigma < \alpha$ and $\tau > \tau^*$:
Original Variables

– – – – – Capital-Rich

————— Balanced Endowment

–·–·–·– Capital-Poor

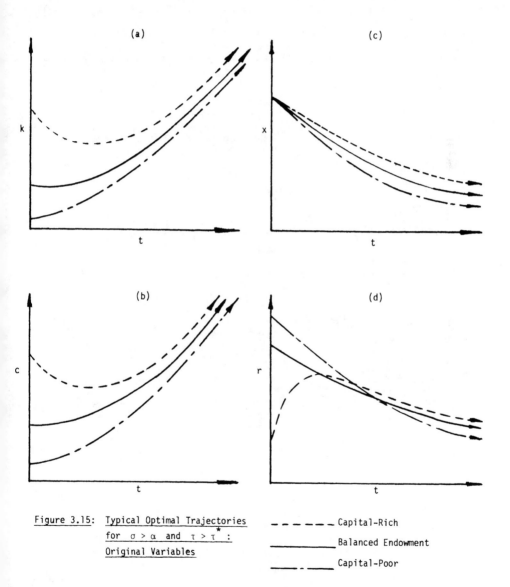

Figure 3.15: Typical Optimal Trajectories
for $\sigma > \alpha$ and $\tau > \tau^{*}$:
Original Variables

- - - - - Capital-Rich

——————— Balanced Endowment

—·—·—· Capital-Poor

3.2.4 Numerical Examples

To illustrate the crucial role of technical progress we return, once again, to the example in Section 3.1.3.

For the parametric values assumed in that example, the minimum critical rate of technical progress τ^* is 0.0015 Thus, any technical progress exceeding 0.15% annually will be enough to sustain an ever improving standard of living.[20]

Summarized below are the various parameters along the balanced endowment paths, assuming $\tau = 0.02$ and $k_*^\tau = 5.0$. Also given, for easy reference, are the same parameters for $\tau = 0$; i.e., the parameters for the static technology.

Parameter	$\tau = 0$	$\tau = 0.02$
x_*^τ	234.0	96,520
k_*^τ	5.0	5.0
c_*^τ	1.220	1.620
r_*^τ	2.34	965.2
$\gamma_k^\tau = \gamma_c^\tau$	-0.002	0.025
$\gamma_x^\tau = \gamma_r^\tau$	-0.030	-0.030
s	0.219	0.226
$\check{\delta}$	0.028	0.055

---

[20]The empirical evidence on the rate of technical progress in the past, is somewhat mixed. The early estimates by Abramovitz [2], Kendrick [15] and Solow [36] attributed a major part of the growth in per capita output to technical progress. Their estimates placed the annual rate of progress for the United States during the last few decades to be between 1 - 2%. However, recently Jorgenson and Griliches [14] have suggested that almost none of the growth in output is attributable to technical progress.

Among the things to be noted are

i) The per capita capital and consumption (and also output) increase at the rate of 2.5% annually. In gross terms, this corresponds to an annual growth rate of 4.5% For comparison, the optimal steady state growth rate in the conventional neo-classical formulation (assuming $\beta = 0$) would have been 4.7% annually.[21] Thus, the introduction of the exhaustible resource in the production function results in a marginal decline of the 'natural growth rate.'

ii) The introduction of technical progress leaves the savings ratio s practically unchanged.

iii) The monetary interest rate $\bar{\delta}$ increases from 0.028 to 0.055 which is larger than δ .

iv) The balanced endowments are highly sensitive to τ. The balanced resource reserves corresponding to a fixed capital stock increase from 234 units for the static technology case to about 96,520 units in case of technical progress at the rate of 2% per annum.

v) As in the case of static technology, the per capita resource usage rate declines at an annual rate of 3%. Even after accounting for the increasing population, the gross usage rate still declines 1% annually.[2]

---

[21]The growth rate would be
$$= n + \frac{\tau}{1-\alpha} \approx 0.047$$
See Arrow and Kurz [4].

[22]In contrast the global usage rates for most exhaustible resources have been growing about 5% annually [40].

Partially at least, the divergence is a result of a definitional dis-crepency. In our model the resource usage rate is specified in actual terms rather than in effective terms. As one of the consequences of tech-nical progress is to increase the effectiveness of a given resource stock

3.3 A Brief Summary

Following is a brief resumé of the analysis and the results of this chapter.

We began by showing that if the production function was of the Cobb-Douglas type and if the utility function had a constant elasticity, then there existed a set of initial endowments from which the optimal solution was of a particularly simple form. Along such a solution, capital, consumption and output all changed at the same exponential rate; the savings rate remained constant and the resource usage rate declined exponentially.

We showed further that the optimal solution starting from an arbitrary initial endowment eventually behaved as if it had originated from some endowment belonging to the special set.

We termed the endowment belonging to the special set, the 'balanced endowment.' It was shown that the balanced capital and resource endowment were related to each other through a unique, monotonically increasing function and that they provided a simple way to determine whether an economy was relatively better endowed with capital or with the exhaustible resource.

(e.g., through better extraction technology, through better utilization and through new discoveries) the effective resource quantity corresponding to some original quantity, grows over time. Thus a resource augmenting technical change at the rate of about 6% per annum would completely explain the discrepency. (Notice that in the present case, a 6% resource augmenting progress is equivalent to a 0.30% Hicks natural progress.) The apparently high figure of 6% may not be too unusual; my crude estimates indicate that for the past few decades, the usable BTU content of the global energy reserves has grown at an annual rate of about 10%.

Additionally, however, the current trend may merely be a part of a transient phase for balancing the originally unbalanced endowments (c.f. Figures (14d) and (15d)); in that case, a reversal of the existing growth trends can be expected, once the original imbalance is eliminated.

Detailed analysis of the optimal solutions from arbitrary initial endowments resulted in two important departures from the traditional optimal growth models: (a) it was possible now to have non-monotonic convergence to the steady state; and (b) the relationship between σ, the elasticity of marginal utility of consumption and α, the elasticity of output w.r.t. the capital, played an important role in determining the qualitative nature of optimal growth trajectories. It was shown, for example, that if two economies started with the same resource endowment but different capital endowments, then the initial resource usage rate for the economy with higher capital, would be higher or lower than that for the other economy, accordingly as $\sigma < \alpha$ or $\sigma > \alpha$.

The results corresponding to $\sigma < \alpha$ were especially interesting because of their somewhat counter-intuitive nature. We showed that if $\sigma < \alpha$ then in the long run, an economy starting from (k_0', x_0) would be better off than another economy which started from (k_0'', x_0) provided $k_0'' > k_0'$.

Lastly, technical progress was introduced into the model and was found to play a crucial role. It was shown that there existed a minimum critical rate of technical progress such that if the actual progress rate were to exceed that, then the economy could sustain an ever improving standard of living despite the limitation imposed by the finiteness of the resource stock. Alternatively, if the rate of progress was below the minimum critical rate then, as in the case of static technology, the economy eventually declined to the null steady state.

91

CHAPTER IV

OPTIMAL GROWTH PATHS UNDER MAX-MIN WELFARE FUNCTIONAL

4.1 Introduction

The preceding analysis, like much of the other literature on optimal growth theory, was utilitarian in the sense that the social welfare functional was defined as a weighted sum of the utilities of the various generations. Such an approach to social choice has come under strong attack recently from John Rawls [28]. He argues that the appropriate goal for a society should be the maximization of the welfare of the least fortunate thus, in effect, ruling out the possibility of trading off the losses of some against the gains of the other. Unlike a utilitarian, a Rawlsian would try to maximize the lowest individual utility.

Rawls restricts his argument primarily to intra-temporal decisions. In an interesting follow-up paper, Solow [37] has tried to analyse the implications of using the Rawlsian max-min criterion in optimal growth models. Solow finds that the use of a welfare functional like[1]

$$W = \min_{0 \le t < \infty} [c(t)] \qquad (4.1)$$

would be reasonable except for two important difficulties: (a) it requires an initial capital stock big enough to support a decent standard of living, else it perpetuates poverty; and (b) it seems to give foolishly conservative injunctions when there is stationary population and exponential technical progress. More pertinent to this study is his conclusion that

---

[1]Implicit in this formulation of the Rawlsian criterion is the assumption that at any time the total consumption is shared equally by the population.

92

the introduction of exhaustible resources into this sort of optimization model leaves the above results unchanged.

Our goal in this chapter is to extend Solow's analysis and to integrate it with the results from the last chapter. We shall show that the differences resulting from the use of the Rawlsian functional (4.1), instead of the conventional utilitarian functional (2.10) are more apparent than real. In fact, for the Cobb-Douglas Technology, we shall show that given technology parameters α and β and given the rate of technical progress τ , the Rawlsian criterion merely represents some specific choice for the discount rate δ Accordingly, we shall argue that the appropriate test for the suitability of using the Rawlsian criterion should be the reasonableness of the implicit δ.

4.2 The Max-min Model

Assuming Cobb-Douglas Technology with Hicks neutral technical progress, the planning problem under the Rawlsian criterion can be stated as

$$\underset{\{c(t)\, ,\, r(t)\}}{\text{Max } W} = \underset{0 \le t \le \infty}{\text{Min}} \quad [c(t)] \qquad \text{(a)}$$

subject to

$$\dot{k} = e^{\tau t} k^{\alpha} r^{\beta} - (\mu+n)k - c \qquad \text{(b)}$$

$$\dot{x} = - (r+nx) \qquad \text{(c)}$$

$$k(0) = k_0 \, , \, x(0) = x_0 \text{ and } r \ge 0, c \ge 0.^2$$

$$\left. \right\} \quad (4.2)$$

---

[2]c.f. Eq. (2.13) for the utilitarian case.

To obtain the necessary conditions for (4.2), we use an approach suggested by Solow [37] for this kind of problem. He points out that except for some trick problems, the optimality according to the max-min criterion requires that the consumption stream be held constant at all times. Accordingly we arbitrarily fix c and then solve the alternate problem

$$
\left.
\begin{aligned}
&\underset{\{r(t)\}}{\text{Min}} \; \xi = \int_0^\infty r \, L \, dt = \int_0^\infty r e^{nt} \, dt \\
&\text{subject to} \quad \dot{k} = e^{\tau t} k^\alpha r^\beta - (\mu+n)k - c \\
&\qquad\qquad k(0) = k_0 \quad \text{and} \quad r \geq 0
\end{aligned}
\right\} \qquad (4.3)
$$

If the minimized value of the integral is greater than the original resource endowment x_0 , then the chosen c was too high and must be reduced; if the minimized value of the integral is less than x_0 , then c was too small and can be increased. When a $c = c_0$ is found for which the minimized value of the integral is exactly x_0 , the original problem is solved.

The necessary optimality conditions for (4.3) can be obtained through the use of the Pontryagin's Maximum principle [4, 26, 34]. The current value Hamiltonian for the problem is given by

$$
H = -r + \lambda[e^{\tau t} k^\alpha r^\beta - (\mu + n)k - c] \qquad (4.4)
$$

where λ is the adjoint variable representing the shadow price of capital in terms of the resource.

For optimality

$$
\frac{\partial H}{\partial r} = 0 = -1 + \lambda e^{\tau t} \beta k^\alpha r^{\beta-1} \qquad (4.5)
$$

94

and

$$\frac{\dot{\lambda}}{\lambda} = -n - \frac{\partial H}{\partial k} = -n - [\alpha e^{\tau t} k^{\alpha-1} r^{\beta} - (\mu + n)]$$

$$= \mu - \alpha e^{\tau t} k^{\alpha-1} r^{\beta} \qquad (4.6)$$

Differentiating (4.5) w.r.t. time logarithmically

$$\frac{\dot{\lambda}}{\lambda} + \tau + \alpha \frac{\dot{k}}{k} + (\beta - 1) \frac{\dot{r}}{r} = 0$$

Substituting from (4.3b) and (4.6)

$$\frac{\dot{r}}{r} = \frac{1}{1 - \beta} [\mu + \tau - \alpha(\mu + n) - \alpha \frac{c}{k}] \qquad (4.7)$$

Also the transversality condition is

$$\lim_{t \to \infty} \lambda(t) \geq 0 \quad \text{and} \quad \lim_{t \to \infty} \lambda(t) \, k(t) = 0 \qquad (4.8)$$

The first part of (4.8) follows trivially from (4.5) while for the second part we must have

$$\lim_{t \to \infty} e^{-\tau t} k^{1-\alpha} r^{1-\beta} = 0 \qquad (4.9)$$

Finally for optimally chosen c we would have

$$x_0 = \int_0^{\infty} r e^{nt} \, dt \qquad \text{so that}$$

$$\dot{x} = -(r + nx), \quad x(0) = x_0, \quad x(\infty) = 0 \quad (4.10)$$

Thus, in addition to the transversality condition (4.9), the optimal solution to (4.2) should satisfy the following:

95

$$\frac{\dot{k}}{k} = e^{\tau t} k^{\alpha-1} r^{\beta} - (\mu + n) - \frac{c}{k} \qquad (a)$$

$$\frac{\dot{x}}{x} = - \left(\frac{r}{x} + n\right) \qquad (b)$$

$$c = c_0 \rightarrow \frac{\dot{c}}{c} = 0 \qquad (c)$$

and $\quad \frac{\dot{r}}{r} = \frac{1}{1 - \beta} \left[(\mu + \tau) - \alpha(\mu + n) - \alpha \frac{c}{k} \right] \quad (d)$

$\left.\begin{array}{c} \\ \\ \\ \\ \\ \\ \\ \\ \end{array}\right\}$ (4.11)

Notice that except for equation (c), the system of equations (4.11) is exactly the same as (3.67) which we obtained for the utilitarian case. As one might expect the analysis of (4.11) closely resembles that of (3.67). Accordingly, in the following discussion the details will be kept to a minimum.

4.3 Analysis of Optimality Conditions

Through an analysis identical to that in Section 3.1.2 of the last chapter, we can show that if the initial endowments k_0 and x_0 were such that

$$x_0 = \frac{1}{\left(\frac{\tau}{\beta} - n\right)} \cdot \left[\frac{\mu + \tau/\beta}{\alpha} \right]^{\frac{1}{\beta}} \cdot k_0^{\frac{1-\alpha}{\beta}} \qquad (4.12)$$

then (4.11) has a simple solution of the form

$$k(t) = \tilde{k}_*$$

$$c(t) = \tilde{c}_*$$

$$r(t) = \tilde{r}_* e^{\gamma_r t}$$

and $\qquad x(t) = \tilde{x}_* e^{\gamma_x t}$

$\left.\begin{array}{c} \\ \\ \\ \\ \end{array}\right\}$ (4.13)

96

where $\tilde{k}_* \ldots \tilde{x}_*$, $\tilde{\gamma}_r$, $\tilde{\gamma}_x$ are constants given by

$$\tilde{\gamma}_r = \tilde{\gamma}_x = -\frac{\tau}{\beta}$$

$$\tilde{k}_* = k_0 \; , \; \tilde{x}_* = x_0$$

$$\tilde{c}_* = \left[\frac{\mu + \frac{\tau}{\beta}}{\alpha} - (\mu + n) \right] \tilde{k}_*$$
(4.14)

and

$$\tilde{r}_* = (\frac{\tau}{\beta} - n)\tilde{x}_*$$

Equation (4.12), in effect, defines the balanced endowments in the Rawlsian sense.[3] It is easy to show that a balanced endowment solution will always satisfy the transversality condition (4.9) and hence will be the optimal Rawlsian solution. Thus starting from a balanced endowment, the optimal solution is to maintain consumption and capital constant and to let the technical progress compensate for the declining resource usage.[4]

---

[3]For (4.12) to be meaningful it is necessary that $\frac{\tau}{\beta} > n$; this constraint is the Rawlsian counterpart to the convergence constraint

$$\frac{\delta(1 - \alpha)}{1 - \alpha - \beta(1 - \alpha)} > n + \tau(1 - \sigma)$$

in the utilitarian formulation. (c.f. footnote 16, Chapter III). Solow [37] has obtained an explicit solution for the limiting case in which $\mu = n = \tau = 0$. I have not proved it but I believe that his solution can be obtained as a limiting form of our general solution. Notice that for $\mu = n = \tau = 0$ the balanced capital endowment $\tilde{k}_*$ corresponding to any finite resource endowment $\tilde{x}_*$ will be infinitely large. As we shall show in the next section, in the long run, the optimal solution from any arbitrary endowment asymptotically approaches the balanced endowment solution. Thus for Solow's limiting case our analysis would predict an infinitely large capital stock, in the long run. The solution obtained by Solow shows that this is, indeed, the case.

[4]We noted previously, that a Hicks neutral technical change at the rate τ could also be considered as a resource augmenting technical change

From (4.13) and (4.14), it can be shown further that along the optimal path, both the output and the savings rate remain constant, the latter being given by

$$s = \frac{\alpha(\mu + n)}{\mu + \frac{\tau}{\beta}} \qquad (4.15)$$

Comparing (4.12) with (3.70), the equation defining the balanced endowment in the utilitarian framework, it is obvious that, in general, the Rawlsian balanced endowments will be different from the utilitarian ones. However, if in the utilitarian formulation we were to choose the discount rate δ such that

$$\delta = \frac{\tau}{\beta} \qquad (4.16)$$

then the two balanced endowment relationships will be the same. Furthermore, in that case, the solutions for the two formulations will completely overlap.[5] Hence if the original endowments were balanced in the Rawlsian sense, then the optimal Rawlsian solution would be the same as the optimal utilitarian solution in which δ and σ are as in equation (4.16). The importance of this result will be evident once we have analyzed the optimal Rawlsian solution corresponding to arbitrary initial endowments.

---

at the rate of τ/β. Thus, while the nominal stock of the resources is being exhausted at a rate $|\gamma_x| = \tau/\beta$, the technical progress exactly compensates for it, and the effective resource stock remains unchanged.

[5] c.f. equations (4.12) - (4.14) and (3.68) - (3.72).

4.4 Optimal Trajectories From Arbitrary Endowments

To characterize the optimal solution corresponding to arbitrary endowments (k_0, x_0), we define new variables, $\tilde{k}_1 \ldots \tilde{r}_1$, normalized with respect to the parameters along some balanced (Rawlsian) endowment, i.e.,

$$\left.\begin{array}{l} k(t) = \tilde{k}_1(t) \cdot \tilde{k}_* \\[2mm] x(t) = \tilde{x}_1(t) \cdot \tilde{x}_* \, e^{\tilde{\gamma}_x t} \\[2mm] c(t) = \tilde{c}_1(t) \cdot \tilde{c}_* \\[2mm] \text{and} \quad r(t) = \tilde{r}_1(t) \cdot \tilde{r}_* \, e^{\tilde{\gamma}_r t} \end{array}\right\} \quad (4.17)$$

The normalized variables are chosen so as to satisfy the initial endowment specifications, i.e.,

$$\left.\begin{array}{l} k_0 = \tilde{k}_1(0) \cdot \tilde{k}_* \\[2mm] \text{and} \quad x_0 = \tilde{x}_1(0) \cdot \tilde{x}_* \end{array}\right\} \quad (4.18)$$

Substituting (4.17) in (4.11) and simplifying we get

$$\frac{\dot{\tilde{k}}_1}{\tilde{k}_1} = \frac{\mu + \frac{\tau}{\beta}}{\alpha}\left[\tilde{k}_1^{\alpha-1}\,\tilde{r}_1^{\beta} - 1\right] + \frac{\tilde{c}_*}{\tilde{k}_*}\left[1 - \frac{\tilde{c}_1}{\tilde{k}_1}\right] \qquad (a)$$

$$\frac{\dot{\tilde{x}}_1}{\tilde{x}_1} = \left(\frac{\tau}{\beta} - n\right)\left[1 - \frac{\tilde{r}_1}{\tilde{x}_1}\right] \qquad\qquad\qquad (b)$$

$$\tilde{c}_1 = \tilde{c}_1(0) \qquad\qquad\qquad\qquad\qquad\qquad (c)$$

$$\frac{\dot{\tilde{r}}_1}{\tilde{r}_1} = \frac{\alpha}{1-\beta}\cdot\frac{\tilde{c}_*}{\tilde{k}_*}\left[1 - \frac{\tilde{c}_1}{\tilde{k}_1}\right] \qquad\qquad (d)$$

$$\left.\begin{array}{c} \\ \\ \\ \\ \\ \\ \end{array}\right\} \quad (4.19)$$

Notice that (4.19) is very similar to (3.37), the normalized

99

system for the utilitarian problem. In fact, if in (3.37) we were to use $\delta = \frac{\tau}{\beta}$ and $\sigma = \frac{\alpha + \beta}{\beta}$ then except for equation (c), the two systems would be identical. The steady state of (4.19) is

$$\tilde{c}_1^\infty = \tilde{k}_1^\infty , \quad \tilde{r}_1^\infty = \tilde{x}_1^\infty \quad \text{and} \quad \tilde{r}_1^\infty = (\tilde{x}_1^\infty)^{\frac{1-\alpha}{\beta}} \qquad (4.20)$$

which is identical to the steady state for (3.37).

The behavior of the normalized variables, during their approach to the steady state can be analyzed through phase diagrams in the $(\tilde{k}_1 , \tilde{r}_1)$ plane and the $(\tilde{r}_1 , \tilde{x}_1)$ plane. A typical diagram in the $(\tilde{k}_1 , \tilde{r}_1)$ plane, for a fixed $\tilde{c}_1$, is shown in Figure 4.1. It can be shown that along the optimal trajectory $\tilde{k}_1$ and $\tilde{r}_1$ will approach the steady state in a unique manner, as shown by the heavy lines in Figure 4.1, i.e., $\dot{\tilde{k}}_1$ and $\dot{\tilde{r}}_1$ will have the opposite signs.

A typical phase diagram in the $(\tilde{r}_1 , \tilde{x}_1)$ plane will be similar to the one for (r_1 , x_1) as shown in Figure 3.4 of the last chapter. Qualitatively, the dynamic behavior of $\tilde{r}_1$ and $\tilde{x}_1$ will be identical to that for r_1 and x_1 . Thus along the optial trajectory $\dot{\tilde{r}}_1$ and $\dot{\tilde{x}}_1$ will have the same sign.

It can be shown that corresponding to any $(\tilde{k}_1(0) , \tilde{x}_1(0))$ there exist unique values of $\tilde{c}_1(0) = \tilde{c}_1$ and $\tilde{r}_1(0)$ such that the trajectories starting at $(\tilde{k}_1(0) , \tilde{r}_1(0))$ and at $(\tilde{r}_1(0) , \tilde{x}_1(0))$ will uniquely converge to the respective steady states.

Figures 4.2 and 4.3 show the typical optimal trajectories for 'capital-rich' and 'capital-poor' economies (in the Rawlsian sense) in terms of the normalized variables. Figure 4.4 shows the same in terms of the original variables.

As in the utilitarian case when the normalized system (4.19)

100

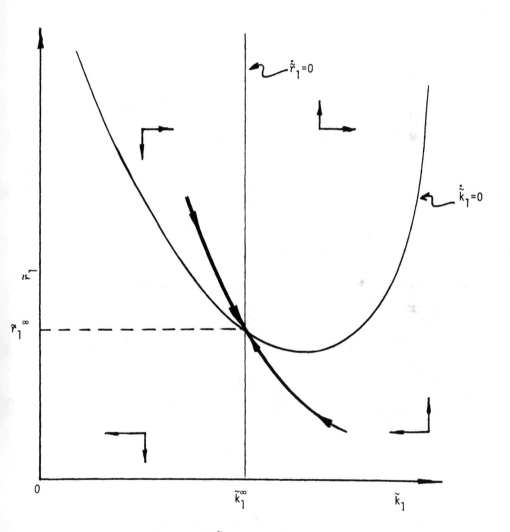

Figure 4.1:   Phase diagram in $(\tilde{k}_1 , \tilde{r}_1)$ plane

101

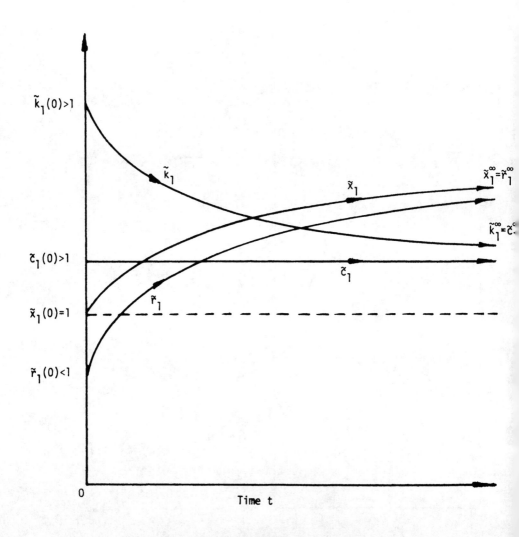

Figure 4.2: Typical Optimal Rawlsian Trajectories for 'Capital-Rich' Economies: Normalized Variables

102

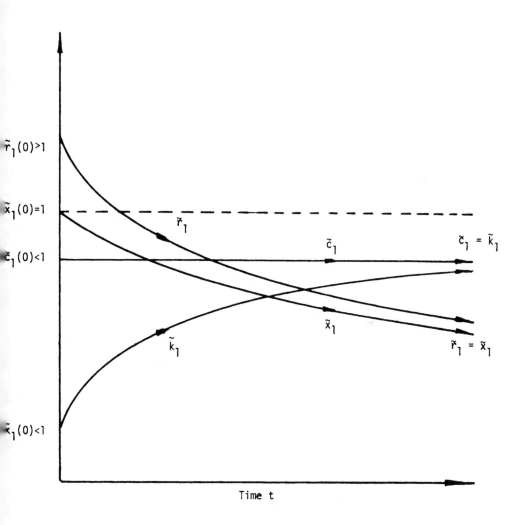

Figure 4.3: Typical Optimal Rawlsian Trajectories for 'Capital-Poor' Economies: Normalized Variables

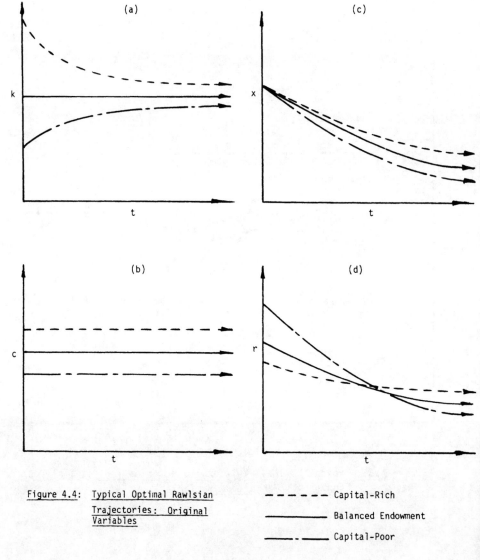

Figure 4.4: Typical Optimal Rawlsian
Trajectories: Original
Variables

------- Capital-Rich

———— Balanced Endowment

—·—— Capital-Poor

104

approaches steady state, (4.17) behaves as if it had started on the balanced endowment locus with initial endowments $\tilde{k}_1^\infty \tilde{k}_*$ and $\tilde{x}_1^\infty x_*$ instead of the arbitrarily specified k_0 and x_0.[6] We noted earlier that starting from a balanced endowment, the optimal Rawlsian solution coincided with the optimal utilitarian solution in which δ was determined in accordance with (4.16). Accordingly, irrespective of the original endowments, the use of the Rawlsian criteron, in the long run, merely implies using the particular values of δ in the utilitarian criterion. Thus, contrary to Solow's conclusion, in the presence of exhaustible resources the suitability of the Rawlsian criterion is essentially independent of the initial capital stock k_0 and depends only on the parameters β and τ.

Intuitively, the devaluation of the role of k_0 can be explained as follows: in the absence of any exhaustible resources in production, the 'transactions' between the current generation and the future generations are constrained by the current capital stock. (The current generation can do no better than to consume all the capital!) The presence of exhaustible resources provides a second vehicle for 'transactions' between the current and the future generations: if the initial capital stock is low ('capital-poor' economy to be more precise), then the current generation can use the resources at a faster pace and vice versa.

The fact that in the present framework a low initial capital stock does not pose any special problems for the Rawlsian criterion

---

[6]Thus along the optimal Rawlsian path k will settle down to a constant value $\tilde{k}_1^\infty \tilde{k}_*$. This is in contradiction to Solow's [37] conjecture that for Rawlsian optimality
$$\lim_{t \to \infty} k(t) = 0$$

should not be construed to imply the suitability of the criterion. In fact, as will be obvious from the following numerical example, the implicit values of δ for most realistic values of the parameters β and τ will be such as to lead to serious questioning of the value judgments implicit in the Rawlsian criterion.[7]

4.5 A Numerical Example

In line with the numerical examples in the last chapter we assume $\alpha = 0.25$, $\beta = 0.05$, $\mu = 0.05$ and $n = 0.02$. Then for the existence of Rawlsian balanced endowments it would be necessary that $\tau > .001$. To bring out the crucial role played by the rate of technical progress in determining the suitability of the Rawlsian criterion, we shall use three different values for τ : .0012, .0015 and .02.[8] Tabulated below are the parameters along Rawlsian balanced endowments for the three cases for $\tilde{x}_* = 1,000$.

---

[7] Interestingly, in a forthcoming publication Rawls [29] agrees that the max-min criterion is unsuitable for inter-temporal decisions.

[8] Recall that $\tau = .0015$ was the minimum critical rate of technical progress in the utilitarian formulation with $\delta = .03$ and $\sigma = 1.0$; for this rate even the utilitarian solution approached constant consumption. We have chosen this value since it provides an easily understood case for comparison between the utilitarian and the Rawlsian criteria. The value $\tau = .0012$ is chosen as typical of the cases where τ is smaller than the critical rate. Lastly the value $\tau = .02$ represents the cases where technical progress exceeds the minimum critical rate.

Parameter	$\tau = .0015$	$\tau = .0012$	$\tau = .02$
$\tilde{x}_*$	1,000	1,000	1,000
$\tilde{k}_*$	5.327	5.562	0.679
$\tilde{c}_*$	1.332	1.256	1.174
$\tilde{r}_*$	10.00	4.00	380.0
$\tilde{\gamma}_r = \tilde{\gamma}_x$	-0.03	0.024	-0.40
s	0.219	0.236	0.039
"δ"	0.03	0.024	0.40

The following two conclusions seem to be obvious from the above table: (i) As in the utilitarian case, the Rawlsian balanced endowments are highly sensitive to the rate of technical progress: An endowment of $k_0 = 2.5$, $x_0 = 1,000$ is 'capital-poor' if $\tau = .0015$ and 'capital-rich' if τ were .02. Thus in the Rawlsian context, a statement that a given capital stock is 'too high' or 'too low' is meaningless; one needs to know, in addition, the accompanying resource stock as well as the anticipated rate of technical progress. (ii) If the actual rate of technical progress is anywhere near 0.02 and β is close to 0.05, then the implicit discount rate in the Rawlsian formulation would be so high as virtually to disquality the criterion. Even if τ were halved and β were doubled, the implicit discount rate would still be 10 percent.

However, if τ were equal to or less than the 'critical' rate of technical progress, then the Rawlsian criterion would seem to be a real alternative to the utilitarian criterion.[9] In fact, if τ were

---

[9]Notice that there is some circularity in this statement since the critical rate of technical progress itself depends upon the choice of δ in the utilitarian criterion.

smaller than the critical rate of .0015 then one might actually prefer the Rawlsian criterion since, unlike the utilitarian criterion, it would ensure a constant non-zero consumption level for ever.

To further illustrate the differences between the two criteria we have shown in Figure 4.5 the trajectories of optimal consumption and resource usage under the two criteria, for initial endowments of k_0 = 2.5 and x_0 = 1,000. The rate of technical progress τ is assumed to be .0015. For the utilitarian case, in line with the numerical example in Section 3.1.3 of the last chapter, we have assumed σ = 1 and δ = .03 .

Figure 4.6 shows the same trajectories for initial endowments of k_0 = 10 and x_0 = 1,000.

If there is a relative capital scarcity (e.g., k_0 = 2.5 and x_0 = 1,000), then the Rawlsian starts with a higher resource usage to compensate for the initial capital deficiency; the utilitarian on the other hand responds by curtailing the initial consumption. In both cases capital is accumulated to overcome the initial deficiency, the rate of accumulation being faster for the utilitarian. By the 13th period, the utilitarian has accumulated enough additional capital to afford a consumption level higher than that of the Rawlsian. The utilitarian consumption continues to increase and asymptotically approaches a value of about 1.39 which is about 7 percent higher than the Rawlsian consumption of 1.30.

If capital is abundant, then the Rawlsian uses the resources more conservatively but the utilitarian has the higher consumption level initially. In both cases the capital is reduced, again the utilitarian doing it more rapidly. By the 17th period the utilitarian has reduced his capital stock so much that his consumption level falls below the

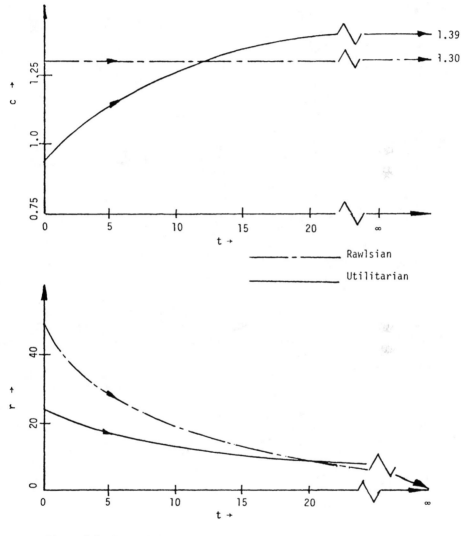

Figure 4.5: Comparison of Optimal Rawlsian and Utilitarian
Trajectories for a 'Capital-Poor' Economy

$$\begin{bmatrix} k_0 = 2.5 \\ x_0 = 1,000 \\ \tau = .0015 \end{bmatrix}$$

109

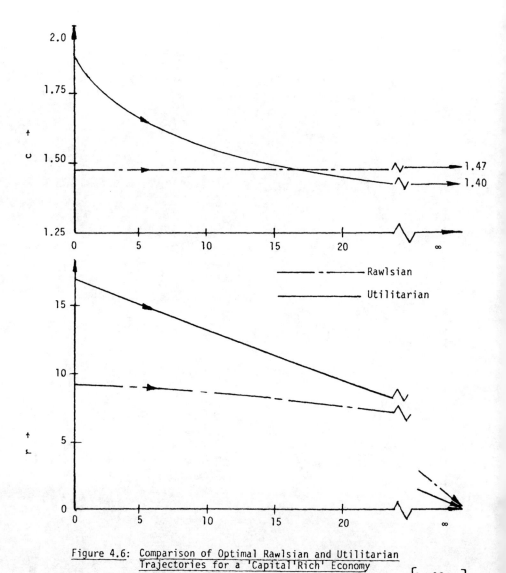

Figure 4.6: Comparison of Optimal Rawlsian and Utilitarian Trajectories for a 'Capital Rich' Economy

$$\begin{bmatrix} k_0 = 10 \\ x_0 = 1,000 \\ \tau = .0015 \end{bmatrix}$$

Rawlsian consumption level. It continues to decrease further and asymptotically approaches a value of about 1.40 which is about 5 percent lower than the Rawlsian level of 1.47.

Thus if capital is relatively scarce, a Rawlsian sacrifices a somewhat higher long term consumption level, in order to maintain a higher consumption level for the few early generations. A utilitarian does the same thing if capital is relatively abundant. Accordingly, as we indicated previously, for τ equal to the critical rate, both criteria would seem to be equally reasonable (or unreasonable).

The situation would be rather different if τ were to be different from the critical rate of technical progress of .0015 If $\tau < .0015$ then for any given initial endowment, there will exist a finite time T such that for all subsequent times the Rawlsian consumption level will be higher than the utilitarian consumption level-- which will approach zero, through exponential decay.

For $\tau > .0015$ the situation will be just the opposite. After some finite time the Rawlsian consumption level will be lower than the exponentially increasing utilitarian level, for all subsequent times.

Thus, the appropriateness of the Rawlsian criterion crucially depends upon the value of τ. If τ is low enough, then the Rawlsian criterion may indeed be preferable to the utilitarian criterion. On the other hand, if τ is large, then Solow's conclusion that for "exponential technical progress the Rawlsian criterion seems to give foolishly conservative injunctions" would be correct.

4.6 A Brief Summary

The primary goal of this chapter has been to evaluate the

suitability of Rawlsian criterion vis-a-vis the utilitarian criterion. In the process of doing so, we showed that the analysis for the Rawlsian case could be carried out along essentially the same lines as for the utilitarian case in Chapter III.

It was shown that as in the utilitarian case, we could define a set of balanced endowments from which the Rawlsian solution was particular simple. Also, we showed that the optimal solution from any other endowment approached this simple solution eventually. We pointed out that the Rawlsian solution from a balanced endowment would overlap with the utilitarian solution if we were to use some specific values for δ and σ in the utilitarian formulation. These values of δ and σ, determined by the technology parameters α, β and τ were, in effect, the implicit utilitarian judgments underlying the Rawlsian criterion, and represented the appropriate parameters for its evaluation. The initial capital endowment was found to be largely irrelevent for evaluating the two criteria.

Lastly, through a numerical example it was shown that if the rate of technical progress were below the 'critical rate', then it would be quite appropriate to use the Rawlsian criterion, while if the rate of progress exceeded the 'critical rate' then the Rawlsian criterion represented extremely conservative value judgments.

112

CHAPTER V
CONCLUSIONS

This chapter summarizes the main conclusions of this study and discusses their relevance to the current debate regarding the use of exhaustible resources. Also discussed in this chapter are the directions for future research, theoretical as well as empirical, needed for further understanding of the various issues.

5.1 Main Conclusions of the Study

Perhaps the most significant conclusion of this study is that even if exhaustible resources are essential to production and there is no technical progress, there need not be any 'sudden catastrophic resource shortage'; when used optimally, the resources will indeed get scarcer over time and the living standard will suffer because of that; however, all this will happen in a gradual fashion. Whether the current allocative mechanisms are operating optimally is beyond the scope of this study; however if they are,then there would be little reason to expect the impending disaster predicted by some recent computer simulaton studies.

Our next major conclusion relates to the optimality of exhausting the resources in a finite time. We showed that even if there were no technical progress, it would be optimal to use up the resources in a finite time unless they are either essential to production or their marginal product becomes unbounded as their usage rate approaches zero. This result would seem to be obvious; we emphasize it here merely because many conservationists have apparently overlooked it. In their writings there is a tendency to assume that because certain usage trends

113

may lead to exhaustion in some finite time, such usage patterns must be non-optimal. The result above would indicate that the mere fact of resource exhaustion in some finite time is not per se an adequate indicator of inter-temporal misallocation.

A related conclusion concerns an often felt but rarely articulated feeling that because mineral deposits are exhaustible, the future returns from them should not be discounted as heavily as the future returns from capital investments. Hotelling [12] and others [11, 31] have already shown this to be incorrect in a partial equilibrium setting; this study shows the same in a more general framework.

We now turn to some of the analytical results specific to the Cobb-Douglas technology.

One of the most significant new concepts to come out of this study is that of 'balanced endowments'. The concept relates to our conclusions that for any economy, there exists a set of capital-resource endowments, defined by a unique monotonic relationship, which are more 'natural' than others. The optimal growth solution starting from these endowments is particularly simple; along such a solution capital, consumption, and output all change at the same exponential rate, the savings rate remains constant, the resource usage rate declines exponentially, and more importantly, the capital stock and the resource stock remain 'balanced' at all times.

The importance of the balanced endowments is underscored by the fact that, in the long run, the optimal solution starting from any arbitrary endowment behaves as if it had started from a balanced endowment, thus, giving a sort of 'turnpike' property to the optimal solution from a balanced endowments.

114

The concept provides a simple way to divide various economies into 'resource-rich' or 'resource-poor' economies[1] and hence a way to compare their relative resource endowments.

The detailed analysis of the optimal growth trajectories, from arbitrarily specified initial endowments, indicates two important departures from the traditional optimal growth models:

(a) It is possible now to have non-monotonic convergence to the steady state; in particular, there exist optimal trajectories along which capital and consumption are increased initially, only to be decreased later on.

This conclusion has a bearing on one of the often expressed conservationist concern that the current living standards in some developed countries have grown too high and can not be maintained for the future generations. The result above indicates that, even if true, such behavior need not be incompatible with optimality.

(b) The relationship between the elasticity of marginal utility of consumption σ and the elasticity of output w.r.t. capital α plays an important role in determining the <u>qualitative</u> nature of the optimal growth trajectories. Thus, for example, if two economies start with the same resource endowment but different capital endowments, then the initial resource usage rate for the economy with the larger capital stock will be higher or lower than that for the other economy accordingly as $\sigma < \alpha$ or $\sigma > \alpha$.

---

[1] By definition they are also 'capital-poor' and 'capital-rich' economies, respectively.

115

The results corresponding to $\sigma < \alpha$ were especially interesting because of their somewhat counter-intuitive nature. We showed that if $\sigma < \alpha$ then in the long run, an economy starting from (k_0', x_0) would be better off than another economy which started from (k_0'', x_0), provided $k_0'' > k_0'$.

This counter-intuitive behavior raises interesting questions about the choice of σ . In so far as the appropriate test for the suitability of an ethical value judgment is the intuitive appeal of its conclusions, the results of this study would seem to suggest restricting σ to be greater than or equal to α .[2]

Not unexpectedly, technical progress was found to play a crucial role in our formulation. It was shown that there existed a minimum critical rate of technical progress such that if the actual progress rate were to exceed that rate, then the economy could sustain an ever improving standard of living, despite the limitations imposed by the finiteness of the resource stock. Alternatively, if the rate of progress were below the critical rate, then the economy must eventually converge to the null steady state. Thus, as our nomenclature implies, the critical rate of technical progress is of critical importance to an economy.

For some plausible values of the model parameters, the critical rate was found to be rather modest-- an annual rate of about 0.2 percent. While the empirical evidence on the rate of technical progress in the

---

[2]However, it ought to be added here that the results from some numerical examples using some plausible values for the various parameters indicate that while the non-monotonic character of optimal trajectories is very significant, the counter intuitive 'rich-poor' reversal is more of an analytical anomaly; in practical terms, its effect is rather insignificant.

past is somewhat mixed, it seems highly unlikely that the rate has been below this critical rate.

Our last few conclusions relate to the optimal behavior under the max-min criterion. The most important conclusion in this regard is that the max-min criterion merely implies using some specific value for the discount rate in the utilitarian criterion. It was shown that the suitability of the max-min criterion, for use in optimal growth models, depended primarily on the technology parameters-- particularly the rate of technical progress. The initial endowments were found to be largely irrelevant in that regard.

It was shown that if the rate of technical progress was below the critical rate then the max-min criterion may indeed be preferable to the utilitarian criterion. For higher progress rates however, the max-min criterion was found to be too conservative.

The result for the case where the rate of technical progress is low does have a bearing on the conservationist controversy. Unlike the utilitarian criterion, the max-min criterion ensures a perpetual non-zero consumption level for some low rates of technical progress. Thus, if the actual rate of progress were below the critical rate, the differences between the conservationists and the economists would repre- sent different value judgments.

5.2 Suggestions for Future Research

The work presented in this study is merely the first step towards a better understanding of the issues involved in inter-temporal usage of exhaustible resources. A lot more work is needed before we have an adequate understanding of the problem. We discuss below some of the areas for future research.

One immediate extension of the work in this study will be to assume a more general production function. Recall that most of our results were derived for a Cobb-Douglas technology. While this represented a major improvement on previous studies, the assumption is still too restrictive. Among other things it implies that the elasticities of substitution between the various factors of production are all equal to one. This in turn implies that the relative shares of the various factors are constant. Thus, it would appear that some of our results may not hold in general. It would be interesting to see the extent to which the results for the Cobb-Douglas case carry over to the more general production functions.[3] Of particular interest would be the fate of the concept of balanced endowments which we found to be so useful in this study.

A second and perhaps more important extension of this study relates to the specification of technical progress. In our formulation technical progress turned out to be the single most important factor in determining the long run behavior of the economy. Considering its importance, the assumption of exogenous technical progress is obviously too simplistic. A more realistic assumption is that technical progress itself is prompted by the economic incentives within the economy: the rate of progress being related to the inputs allocated to research and

---

[3]Preliminary analysis indicates that at least the results about the non-monotonic convergence to the steady state are true for production functions which are considerably more general than the Cobb-Douglas production function.

development. Several recent studies in optimal growth theory have
adopted such a view in order to make technical progress endogenous to
the system.[4] As a start a similar approach could be used in our
formulation.

A further refinement will be to attempt a breakdown of the
catch-all term 'technical progress' into its various components. The
term conceals within itself a variety of different mechanisms with widely
differing dynamics. For example, resource augmenting technical progress
encompasses, among other things, new discoveries, improvements in process
efficiency and the development of new substitutes. It is quite possible
that the 'production function' for creating technical progress would be
quite different for these different mechanism, e.g., one would expect
that the chances of discovering new reserves would depend very signifi-
cantly on the size of the territory previously unexplored, or that the
productivity of research activities devoted to upgrading the efficiency
of a process would depend upon the gap between the actual and the
theoretical limit. Both of these mechanism could be subject to saturation.
On the other hand development of new substitutes does not seem to be
constrained by any such considerations and need not have any saturation
level. Thus, it would be useful to model the various components of
technical progress separately and to analyze the implications of various
mixes of those components.

Another major improvement of this study would be to introduce
uncertainty into the model. Assessing the prospects for future technical

---

[4]See for example, Kennedy [15], Shell [32], and Nordhaus [21].

119

progress is perhaps one of the most speculative areas at this time. Questions such as "Will there be a breeder reactor by a certain date?" or "Shall we be able to harness the fusion process?" are of basic importance for planning future supplies of energy. Answers to such questions must necessarily be in probablistic terms. The dangers of being over optimistic about the prospects of such breakthroughs are obvious enough; less obvious but equally important are the dangers of being too conservative-- one may needlessly conserve something which later on may turn out to be of dubious value. Thus,it would be interesting to see how the optimal policies are affected as we introduce uncertainty into our model.

Yet another improvement in the model would be to introduce the possibility of trade by reformulating it as a two-country problem. One could assume that the two countries have different relative endowments of capital and resource and hence can trade with each other. Possibly such a formulation would lead to a two-person differential game.

Some other extensions of the work in this study would be to assume more than one exhaustible resource or to introduce a separate production function for resource extraction.

Turning to the empirical side, the first priority must go towards obtaining estimates of the role of exhaustible resources in the aggregate production function of the various economies. Estimating the resource augmenting bias of technical progress as well as its breakdown into some sub-groups would be another major contribution. The latter data is important since if we want to make any intelligent guesses about the future course of technical progress on the basis of past trends, we need to understand the mechanism through which the change in the past was brought about.

REFERENCES

1. "A Blueprint for Survival," The Ecologist, Vol. 2, No. 1, (Jan. 1972), pp. 1-42.

2. Abramovitz, M., "Economic Growth in the United States," American Economic Review, 52, (Sept. 1962), pp. 762-782.

3. Anderson, K., "Optimal Growth When the Stock of Resources is Finite and Depletable," Journal of Economic Theory, 4, (April 1972), pp. 256-267.

4. Arrow, K.J., and Kurz, M., Public Investment, the Rate of Return and Optimal Fiscal Policy, Johns Hopkins, Baltimore, 1972.

5. Barnett, H.J. and Morse, C., Scarcity and Growth, John Hopkins, Baltimore, 1969.

6. Burt, O.R. and Cummings, R.G., "Production and Investment in Natural Resource Industries," American Economic Review, 60, (Sept. 1970), pp. 576-590.

7. Cass, D., "Optimum Growth in an Aggregative Model of Capital Accumulation," Review of Economic Studies, Vol. 32, (July 1965), pp. 233-240.

8. Chakarvarty, S., Capital and Development Planning, M.I.T. Press, 1969.

9. Cole, H.S.D., ed. Models of Doom, Universe Books, New York, 1973.

10. Gordon, R.L., "A Reinterpretation of the Pure Theory of Exhaustion," Journal of Political Economy, 75, (June 1967), pp. 274-86.

11. Herfindahl, O.C., "Depletion and Economic Theory", in M. Gaffney, Extractive Resources and Taxation, University of Wisconsin Press, 1967, pp. 63-90.

12. Hotelling, H., "The Economics of Exhaustible Resources," Journal of Political Economy, 39, (April 1931), pp. 137-175.

13. Intriligator, M., Mathematical Optimization and Economic Theory, Prentice Hall Inc., Englewood Cliffs, N.J., 1971.

14. Jorgenson, D. and Griliches, A., "The Explanation of Productivity Change," Review of Economic Studies, 34, (July 1967), pp. 249-284.

15. Kendrick, J.W., Productivity Trends in the United States, Princeton University Press, 1961.

16. Kennedy, C., "Induced Bias in Innovation and the Theory of Distribution," Economic Journal, Vol. 74 (Sept. 1964).

REFERENCES (cont.)

17. Koopmans, T.C., <u>Some Observations on Optimal Economic Growth and Exhaustible Resources</u>, Cowles Foundation Paper No. 396, Yale University, 1973.

18. Lewis, A., <u>The New York Times</u>, January 14, 1972.

19. Malthus, T.R., <u>An Essay on the Principle of Population</u>, Reprint of 6th Ed.; Ward, Lock and Company, London, 1826.

20. Meadows, D.H., et. al. <u>The Limits To Growth</u>, Potomac Associates, Washington, D.C., 1972.

21. Nordhaus, W.D., "World Dynamics; Measurement Without Date," <u>The Economic Journal</u>, Vol. 82, (Dec. 1972) pp. 1156-1183.

22. _____, "The Optimal Rate and Direction of Technical Change" in K. Shell ed. <u>Essays on the Theory of Optimal Economic Growth</u>, M.I.T. Press 1967, pp. 53-66.

23. Nordhaus, W.D. and Tobin, J., <u>Economic Growth; Retrospect and Prospects</u>, 50th Annual Colloquim V, National Bureau of Economic Research, 1972.

24. Passel, P. et. al., <u>The New York Times Book Review</u>, April 2, 1972.

25. Pigou, A.C. <u>The Economics of Welfare</u>,4th Ed. London: MacMillan, 1952.

26. Pontryagin, L.S. et. al., <u>The Mathematical Theory of Optimal Processes</u>, Interscience Publications, New York, 1962.

27. Ramsey, F., "A Mathematical Theory of Savings," <u>Economic Journal</u>, 38, (Dec. 1928), pp. 543-59.

28. Rawls, J., <u>A Theory of Justice</u>, Harvard University Press, 1971.

29. _____, Some Remarks on the Maxi-Min Criterion," Presented at the 86th Annual Meeting of American Economic Association, New York Dec. 1973.

30. Rosenberg, N., "Innovative Responses to Material Shortages," <u>Papers and Proceedings of the 85th Annual Meeting of American Economic Association</u>, Toronto, Canada, Dec. 1972, pp. 111-118.

31. Scott, A., "The Mine Under Conditions of Certainty," in M. Gaffney (ed.) <u>Extractive Resources and Taxation</u>, University of Wisconsin Press, 1967, pp. 25-62.

32. Shell, K., "A Model of Inventive Activity and Capital Accumulation" in K. Shell (ed.), <u>Essays on the Theory of Optimal Economic Growth</u>, M.I.T. Press 1967, pp. 67-85.

33. Shell, K., "Optimal Program of Capital Accumulation For an Economy in Which There is Exogenous Technical Change"in K. Shell ed. Essays on the Theory of Optimal Economic Growth, M.I.T. Press 1967, pp. 1-30.

34. _____, "Applications of Pontryagin's Maximum Principle to Economics," in H.W. Kuhn and P. Szego (eds.) Mathematical Systems Theory and Economics I: Proceedings of the International Summer School in Varenna, Italy, June 1967 .

35. Solow, R.M., "A Contribution to the Theory of Economic Growth," The Quarterly Journal of Economics, Vol. 70, (Feb. 1956), pp. 65-94.

36. _____, "Technical Change and the Aggregative Production Function," Review of Economic Statistics, 39, (August 1957), pp. 312-320.

37. _____,"Intergenerational Equity and Exhaustible Resources," Working Paper No. 103, Dept. of Economics, M.I.T., Feb., 1973.

38. Swan, T.W., "Economic Growth and Capital Accumulation," The Economic Record, XXXII, (Nov. 1956), pp. 334-61.

39. Sweeney, J.L.,"Optimal Extraction of Depletable Resources: Market Forces and Intertemporal Bias," (Unpublsihed paper, Dept. of Engineering-Economics Systems, Stanford University, 1973.

40. U.S. Bureau of Mines, Mineral Facts and Problems, Washington, D.C., 1970.

41. Vousden, N., "Basic Theoretical Issues of Resource Depletion," Journal of Economic Theory, 6, (April 1973), pp. 126-143.